ABERDEEN ● ▲ ─── Crathes

PERTH ●
▲ ─────── Branklyn

GLASGOW ● ● EDINBURGH

Brodick ─── ▲

BELFAST ●
▲   ▲
Mount Stewart
Rowallane

DUBLIN ●

▲ ─── Castle Howard

HARROGATE ●
Harlow Car ─── ▲ ▲ ─── Studley Royal
Harewood House ─── ▲ ● YORK
                    ▲ ─── Bramham
                          Rudding Park

LLANDUDNO ●
Bodnant ─── ▲

▲ ─── Chatsworth
▲ ─── Haddon Hall
DERBY ● ▲ ─── Belton House

SHREWSBURY ●
                          ▲ ─── Alton Towers
Powis Castle ─── ▲   Packwood House
Weston Park   LEICESTER ●
Burford House ─── ▲   ▲ ─── Anglesey
Charlecote ─── ▲ COVENTRY ●   Stowe

Hidcote   STRATFORD ● ▲   ▲ ─── CAMBRIDGE ●
Sudeley ─────────────── ▲ ▲   ▲ ─── Ascott
Blenheim   Wrest Park
Compton Wynyates   ▲
CARDIFF ●   OXFORD ●
Ashridge ──────   LONDON ●
Westonbirt ──────   Cliveden ─── Windsor
                                        Kew
           ▲ ▲ ● SALISBURY   Hampton Court
Knightshayes   TUNBRIDGE WELLS
Killerton Park ─── ▲ ▲   ▲ CANTERBURY ●
East Lambrook   ▲ ▲
Lanhydrock   EXETER ● ▲ BRIGHTON ● Childham
TRURO ●   ▲   Sissinghurst
Glendurgan ─── ▲ WEYMOUTH ●   Scotney
Cotehele   Tintinhull Buscot Park   Chartwell
Dartington Hall Montacute Winkworth   Penshurst
Antony Park   Bicton   Wakehurst   Sheffield Park
                Athelhampton Wisley   Borde Hill
                Stourhead   Nymans
                Compton Acres Polesden Lacey

THE BEAUTIFUL GARDENS OF BRITAIN

A
Golden Hands
book

Marshall Cavendish, London

Photographs by:

Aerofilms Limited: 104B
Amateur Gardening: 64
Belton House Estate: 101C
D. V. Blogg: 62B
Pamela Booth: 19TR, 54B, 59TR
British Travel Association: 59B, 75BR, 76, 77, 87, 93B,
113T, 115T, 116, 117T, 118, 119L, 121R, 123B, 124R
Clark Nelson Limited: 70T
Martin Corbin: 112R
A. de Rahm: 28, 83T, 84, 89C, 126B
G. Douglas-Bolton: 16T, 100, 109T, 123T, 124T, L
Valerie Finnis: 3B, 23BR, 24, 25, 26, 42B, 78
Miles Hadfield: 5TR, 80B
G. Hall: 103
Iris Hardwick: 6BL,R, 11, 12, 13TL, 14, 15B, 16B, 17,
18, 19BR, 20TL, 20TR, 21, 22, 27, 29B, 33, 34, 39,
40B, 70, 71T,BL, 85, 86, 88, 89B, 70, 71T,BL, 92T, 115L
A. G. L. Hellyer: 7TL, 41TR,BL,C, 42TL,TR, 65R, 66T,
69C, 79, 80T, 105, 107, 108B, 111T, 112L, 114B,
125T, 126L,R, 127B, 128
Peter Hunt: 7B, 8, 9, 10, 23T,BL, 47, 48, 71T, 73, 74,
A. J. Huxley: 32 ,38B, 67T
A. F. Kersting: 5B, 31, 44, 52T, 53T, 54T, 56T, 61, 68
Ken Lemmon: 43B, 114R
Charles Lines: 40T, 93T, 94TL,TR, 108T
P. Minay: 51, 52B
Ministry of Public Buildings and Works: 81T, 82B
National Trust/P. Wenham: front cover
S. J. Orme: 55, 56B, 65TL,BL, 66B
D. J. Pearce: 35TR, 36TR,B
Picturepoint: 37T, 38T, 75TR,BL, 95, 96, 109B, 110, 127T
Popperfoto: 71BR, 72, 83B
Ray Procter: 6T, 7TR
Ianthe Ruthven: 29TL,C,TR, 30
Kay Sanecki: 35, 46, 49, 50, 112B
A. D. Schilling: 63T,C
Donald Smith: 81L,TR,BR, 82T
Harry Smith: 15T, C, 19L, 20B, 35TL,B, 57T, 59TL,
62T, 63B, 70BL, 71BL, 89T, 119TR,B, 120, 125B
G. S. Thomas: 43, 67B, 115R
T. G. Thornley: 69T,B, 70BR,
John Treasure: 91BR, 92C
A. Turner: 94B
B. Unne: 104T
T. W. G. Wright: 36TL, 41BR
Map reproduced by courtesy of
John Bartholomew & Son Ltd.
T/top
B/bottom
C/centre
L/left
R/right

Edited by Humphrey Evans

Published by Marshall Cavendish Publications Limited,
58 Old Compton Street, London W1V 5PA.
©Marshall Cavendish Ltd 1968, 1970, 1974

This material was first published by
Marshall Cavendish Limited in the partwork
Encyclopedia of Gardening

This volume first published 1974

Printed by Morrison & Gibb, Edinburgh

ISBN 0 85685 056 X

This volume not to be sold in the USA, Canada and the Philippines

About this book

A beautiful garden gives pleasure to all who see it — and *The Beautiful Gardens of Britain* makes sure that you share this pleasure and enjoy to the full Britain's living heritage of magnificent gardens.

More than 60 famous gardens, each illustrated with two pages of colorful photographs, cover the wide variety of Britain's beautiful gardens. There are details of plants, trees and shrubs, accounts of special features and wonderful vistas, descriptions of garden plans and layouts — everything that makes these British gardens outstanding.

This is a book for the gardener and the garden-lover, the tourist and the holiday-maker—and for the stay-at-home who likes to dream. It is a book you can mull over—looking for ideas to adapt on a smaller scale or deciding on places to visit.

The gardens are listed by areas so that you can use *The Beautiful Gardens of Britain* as a traveller's guide, with its full information about how to get to the gardens, when they are open and what they are noted for.

Contents

Lanhydrock, a garden for all seasons

Unlike most Cornish gardens, Lanhydrock is not situated close to the coast, but well inland overlooking the richly wooded valley of the River Fowey. A plan shows that there was a good garden here in 1694, but the present gardens were laid out from the mid-nineteenth century onwards with considerable alterations and additions in the nineteen-thirties.

The house is reached by a long avenue of Sycamores planted in 1648, and is guarded by the highly decorated seventeenth-century Gatehouse. Around this, and in front of the house itself, the gardens are formal. Neat pyramids of Conifers arise with regularity, and tidy beds of Tulips and Forget-me-nots, followed later by Roses, are within clipped hedges which in turn are guarded from the outside world by Victorian granite walls decorated with finials dated, however, 1657. Here will be found exceptionally fine urns modelled by Louis Ballin, Goldsmith to Louis XIV of France. Against the house itself are good specimens of the evergreen late-flowering *Magnolia grandiflora*, a native of the south-eastern states of the USA.

Right In the Higher Garden at Lanhydrock where many fine specimens of trees and shrubs are grown. *Below* The seventeenth-century Gatehouse, the wall with its seventeenth-century finials and the house.

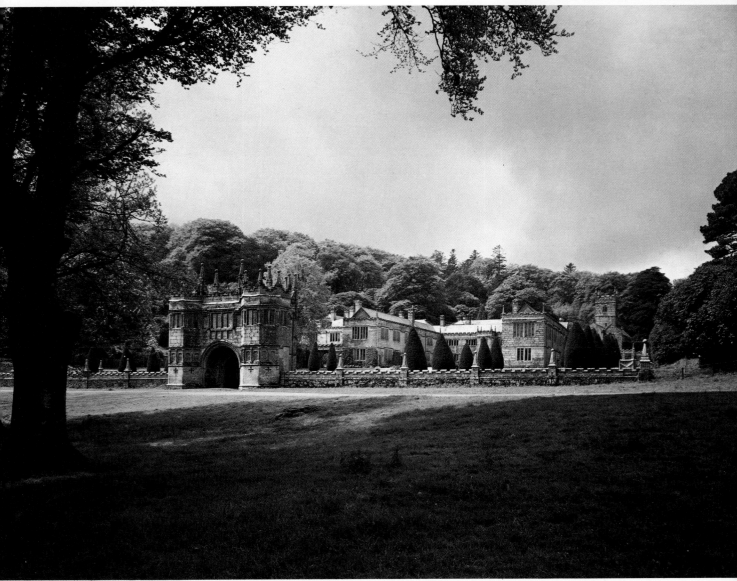

Behind and above the house is the Higher Garden which contains twentieth century plantings of trees and shrubs among older specimens. Among them paths wander around and through them delightful views are obtained of the house and gardens below. There is always something to see. In early spring there are the giant-flowered *Magnolia campbellii* and *M. mollicomata.* Later, a great variety of Himalayan and Chinese Rhododendrons bloom into June, when the astonishing Japanese Dogwood *(Cornus kousa)* is a remarkable sight. There are many Japanese Cherries. Later in the season, Hydrangeas are followed by rich autumn leaf-colour. At all times, fine exotic Conifers, and particularly some majestic Irish Yews, impart a sense of dignity.

This property of the National Trust is open from April to September on Wednesdays and Saturdays from 2 to 6. It is 2½ miles south-east of Bodmin; from A38 turn south at Carminow Cross; from Bodmin or Lostwithiel take B3268. Bus 54 (Lostwithiel, Bodmin, Wadebridge) stops at the gate.

Right Part of the formal garden round the house. *Below left* The seventeenth-century Gatehouse looking inwards to the formal garden. *Below right* One of the urns, surrounded by rose beds.

Glendurgan, a garden in the glen

This famous Cornish garden, now the property of the National Trust, gets its name from the lovely glen which it occupies. This curls downwards from the high ground on which the house stands to the tiny hamlet of Durgan on the eastern side of the Helford River. It is a spot of great natural beauty, sufficiently sheltered and mild to permit the cultivation of many exotic trees and shrubs which grow here as freely as in their native countries.

On the upper lawn, near the house, the visitor is greeted by the great succulent rosettes of a Mexican Agave and in the valley below the rare South American evergreen, *Drimys winteri*, is planted in groves and has grown to tree-like proportions. Rhododendrons and Azaleas of many kinds thrive

Above, left The lawn above the valley with a fine specimen of *Agave americana*. *Above, right* Looking over the wooded slopes to the Helford River. *Right* The house with clumps of Rhododendrons and Azaleas.

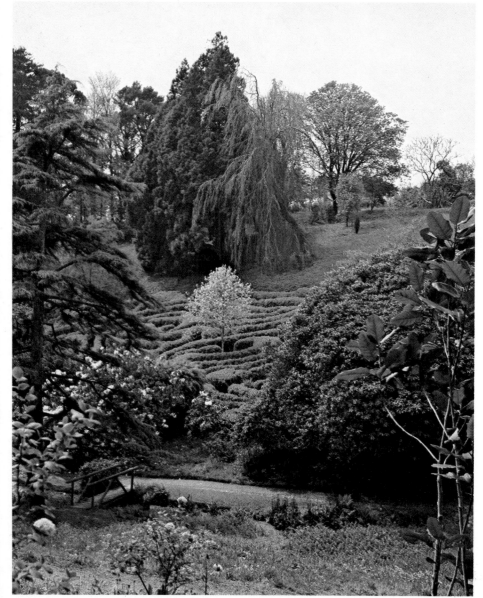

Above, left In May the gassy slopes are thick with Bluebells. *Above, right* Primulas and Gunneras flourish by the water. *Below* The Laurel maze seen from the far side of the valley. The centre-piece is a Whitebeam.

in this valley including a large number of the more tender kinds some of which have richly fragrant flowers. On the damper ground Asiatic Primulas have naturalised themselves and grow as freely as native Primroses.

But in addition to its rare and beautiful plants, Glendurgan possesses an unusual interest in a garden of this type. On the steepest part of the slope below the house is a large maze formed of close-clipped Laurel with a Whitebeam as its centre-piece. From its situation it appears as a complex pattern when viewed from a distance at the far side of the valley, and it also makes an unexpectedly formal feature in this relatively wild section of the garden.

Near the house is a large walled garden, no doubt formerly used for fruit and vegetables but now planted with flowers including many climbing plants. From this point a path leads along the top of the valley to a fine viewpoint over the river estuary.

Glendurgan is 4 miles southwest of Falmouth and the gardens are open on Mondays and Wednesdays from April to September and Fridays in April and May from 10.30 am–4.30 pm.

Antony Park, a Cornish landscape garden

In the late eighteenth century Cornish gardeners found that their climate enabled them to grow, out of doors, a great many plants which, elsewhere in Britain, needed winter protection under glass. This led to a type of garden associated with Cornwall and usually made in Victorian times by one of the old Cornish families.

It incorporated both the remains of the old style and the beginnings of the new, using plant intro-

Above left: the colonnaded entrance to the garden. *Above right:* the remarkable yew 'arbour', clipped to the shape of a perfect cone. *Left:* the Burmese temple bell, a trophy of the nineteenth century Burma wars, flanked by granite lanterns from Japan.

ductions of the late nineteenth and early twentieth centuries.

Antony House, with its interesting interior, was built early in the eighteenth century for Sir William Carew. Its garden is new, the work of Sir William's successor Sir John Carew Pole, and begun in 1945.

The house stands above the tidal estuary of River Lynher, which is seen at the end of vistas framed by giant ilex trees planted in 1760.

Around the house are lawns and topiary, including an extraordinary giant cone in yew.

In the broad alleyway is a large maidenhair tree – the ginkgo – a survivor from prehistoric times. Its remains are found as fossils, and

Painted statues of a shepherd and shepherdess dating from the mid eighteenth century, stand on either side of a garden seat in a recess in the tall, closely clipped yew hedge.

it still grows wild in China.

The new part of the garden forms an arc centred upon the house. It is typical of the modern woodland type but is differentiated by the massing of shrubs and plants usually grown in small numbers. *Pieris forrestii*, whose flaming foliage in spring is as brilliant as any flower, is an example. The hybrid *williamsii* series of camellias, originated by J. C. Williams of Caerhays a little further down the coast by using *C. saluenense* introduced as recently as 1924 from western China as a parent is

also widely planted as are *Rhododendron cinnabarinum* and its hybrids with their bell-like pendant flowers ranging from red through rose to orange. There, too, are masses of the lilac-blue *R. augustinii* and the giant-flowered, heavily scented Loderii hybrids. Magnolias, viburnums, embothriums (the Chilean 'Fire Bush'), Crinodendrum with their crimson lantern-like flowers as well as maples and magnolias are steadily maturing year by year.

Antony House is a National Trust property and is open from April to September from 2 to 6 on Tuesdays, Wednesdays, Thursdays and Bank Holiday Mondays. It is on the A38, five miles west of Plymouth via Torpoint car ferry.

Cotehele, tender plants in an ancient setting

The route to Cotehele lies through winding Cornish lanes, emerging under ancient sycamores. There the squat, grey medieval tower of this ancient place rises from a cluster of granite buildings. Standing on a small plateau, with the River Tamar not far away below, it is possible to see the banks on the opposite side through the tops of the trees lower down a small valley.

Near the house are conventional flower beds set in the grass. On and around the old walls, in sheltered corners, are trees and shrubs. There is the silver wattle (*Acacia dealbata*) from the Australian continent, with silvery leaves and scented yellow flowers that open early in the year. The evergreen Macartney rose *(Rosa bracteata)* (so called be-

Above left and left: The old dovecote or columbarium with some of the many rhododendrons which are a feature of the garden. *Above right:* A white wisteria by a door in the wall.

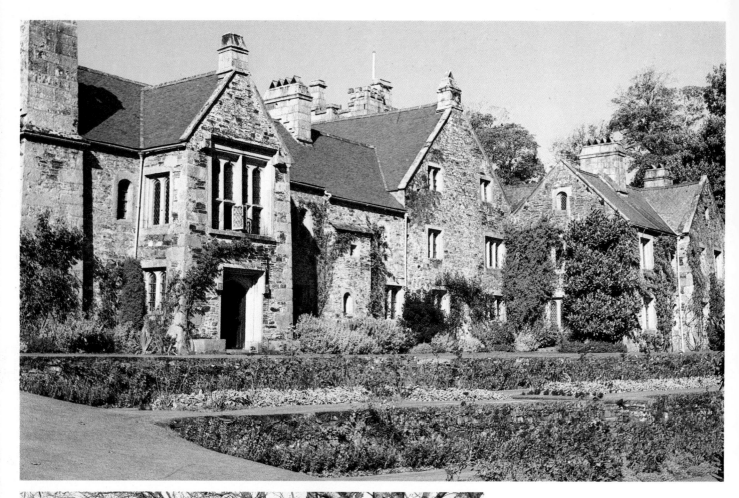

cause it was brought from China in 1793 by Lord Macartney) climbs up a wall— a giant in every way (including its thorns) bearing its large white single flowers over a long period.

A short tunnel leads into a garden planted with greater informality. At its head a pond is the principal feature: from it a stream overflows and tumbles down the valley. On the damp margins waterside plants such as primulas, irises and gunnera, with leaves that may be six feet across, are found. Here, too, is a remarkable building with a domed roof, which is a medieval dove-cot. The banks either side are planted in a typical Cornish manner with rhododendrons, azaleas, maples, bamboos, and hardy palms.

Cotehele is a National Trust property. It is on the west bank of the Tamar, 2 miles of Calstock by footpath or 6 miles by road. It is 8 miles south-west of Tavistock.

It is open from April to September daily, except Tuesdays, from 10 to 6 and from October to March on Wednesdays, Saturdays, Sundays and Bank Holiday Mondays from 2 to 6 or dusk if earlier.

Above: The ancient house, its walls supporting many plants. and part of the terraced garden.
Below: The approach to the house in spring.

Dartington Hall, modern sculpture in a medieval setting

Dartington Hall was built in the fourteenth century by John Holland, Duke of Exeter, a jouster of international fame. The site of his tournament ground has now been turned into a lawn set against the ruins of old buildings. On it stands an effective line of Irish Yews, the 'Twelve Apostles', while around it are some very ancient Sweet Chestnuts and on the bank above (now a series of grass terraces, so making the old Tilt Yard into an open-air theatre) is a magnificent Monterey Pine. At the end of the terrace is a great flight of steps leading through a Heath Garden.

The rest of the garden, on an undulating slope, is largely designed around a number of magnificent old trees—Beeches, London Planes, Cedars, Tulip Trees, Holm and Lucombe Oaks, and a giant Turkey Oak. Among them have been planted glades of newer trees and shrubs. By the Azalea Dell is a round pond in which two swans carved in granite stand on an old cider mill; elsewhere contemporary sculpture is most effectively placed, notably Henry Moore's 'Reclining Woman'.

Walking around the wide and winding grass paths, one finds fine Magnolias, Cherries and Rhododendrons well as an exceptionally large Handkerchief Tree. This fine modern garden in a setting of ancient buildings and trees was begun after the First World War and was designed by an American, Mrs Beatrix Farrand, with later additions by Mr P. S. Cane.

Dartington Hall lies about one mile out of Totnes, Devon on the A384 in the direction of Ashburton. The garden is open all the year round but a permit must be obtained for coach or large parties.

1 A contemporary sculpture by Henry Moore is a twentieth-century addition to the old garden. 2 A flight of steps at the end of the terrace. 3 A rhododendron lined path leads to the tower of a derelict church. 4 The line of Irish Yews known as the 'Twelve Apostles'. In spring the building can be seen through the trees.

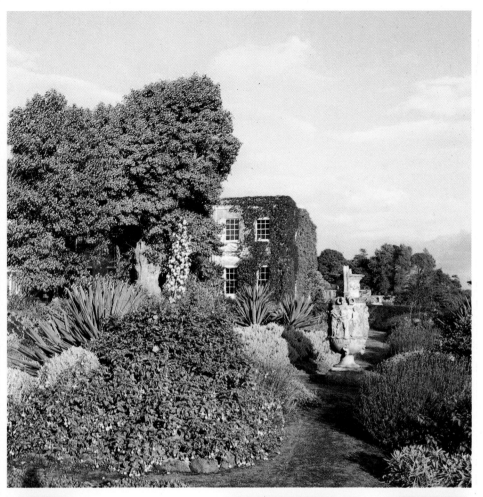

Killerton, unusual tender plants

Killerton Park is first visible as a hill which, even from a distance, is clearly seen to be planted with trees that are not usually seen in the English landscape. The hill is of acid volcanic soil in which rhododendrons and other lime-haters thrive. The climate is mild and border-line trees such as eucalyptus grow quite happily.

The Aclands have lived in the district since the early fifteenth century. It was Sir Thomas Acland, the tenth baronet, who, well aware of the excellence of his site and the fact that he could grow tender plants, began the garden just after the Napoleonic wars. He engaged a local nurseryman, Robert Veitch, a Scot. Veitch later moved to Exeter and the family firm that he established was, until the beginning of the present century, the outstanding introducer of plants from America and China.

Entering the grounds above the house (which is not open to the public), one is led below the hill, passing some exceptionally fine specimens of trees and rhododendrons scattered among the grass. Then the climb begins, passing a Victorian rustic summerhouse, called the 'Bear House' because a bear was once kept in it. The floor is laid with the knucklebones of deer. Above it is an old rock-garden below which is an Ice House dating from the mid-nineteenth century. Up on the hill, with its wide views to Dartmoor, there are several paths. There is a walk by great beech trees, below which are large cork oaks. High up, there is a rhododendron glade

Above: The mild climate of Devonshire encourages luxuriant growth, and tender plants.
Below: In spring the vista over the distant hills extends the natural beauty of Killerton.

15

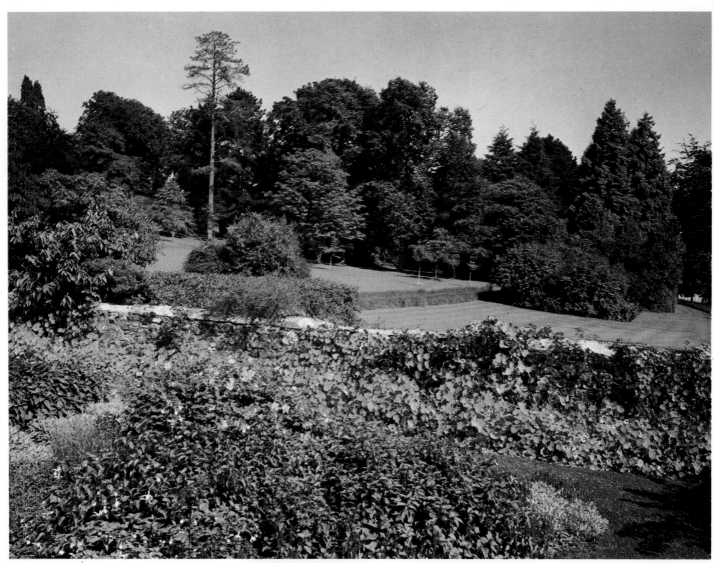

and on the edge of the grounds, a band of azaleas in blazing colours. In spring, there are masses of daffodils. Following the guide, exceptional specimens of magnolia, many rare conifers, the flaming embothrium from South America and eucalyptus from the Australian continent may be seen. There is also one of the largest tulip trees in Britain.

In this mild climate there is much to be seen very early in the year, and thence onward throughout the seasons. Autumn is a particularly pleasant time to see the gardens, as the leaves of many of the trees colour beautifully before they fall. Killerton Park is reached by a minor road (B3185) branching off to the left, 7 miles north of Exeter on A38. The gardens, which belong to the National Trust, are open daily throughout the year.

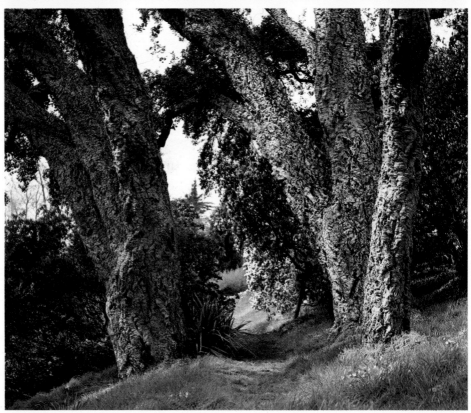

Above: Annuals add colour and a sense of profusion to the garden in summer. *Below:* The old grey trunks of the Cork Oaks, in Killerton Gardens.

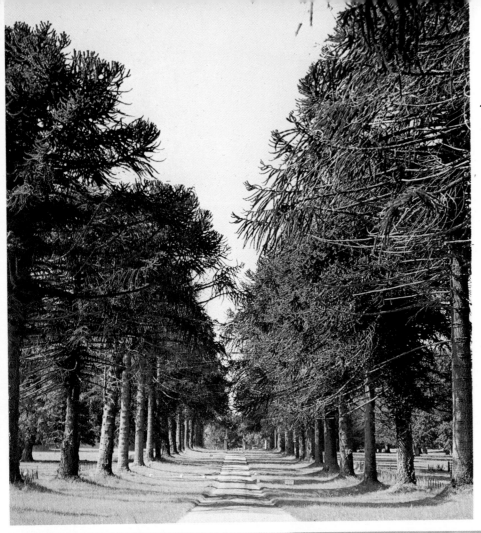

Bicton, three gardens in one

The gardens at Bicton consist of three distinct areas, the so-called Italian Garden, the American Garden and the Pinetum.

The first is said to have been designed in the style of Le Nôtre in the eighteenth century. It is still formal in design, with a rectangular pool, a fountain and a canal, but now Victorian in character, with its dominating Deodars and other conifers. Above it, at one end, stand the range of glasshouses with a Temple at their centre, and, somewhat detached, the handsome Palm House. These contain a most interesting

Left: A long avenue of Monkey Puzzles (Araucarias). *Below:* The Temple at the centre of a row of glasshouses containing an interesting range of plants, all clearly labelled.

range of plants all clearly labelled.

From this range of houses a good view is obtained of the formal lay-out while to the left of it is the American garden for which there was a vogue early in the last century in which were grown many trees shrubs and plants introduced from North America. Here too there is much to see all the year round with many fine specimens including the rare Mexican or Montezuma Pine as well as Rhododendrons and Azaleas in the spring.

The Pinetum originally laid out in 1830 and subsequently added to particularly in 1910 when many of the then new introductions from western China were added, contains one of the most remarkable collections of conifers in the British Isles. Among its sombre shades are majestic specimens of record size and rarities seldom grown elsewhere in Britain.

Beyond the Pinetum lies the Hermitage a nineteenth century summer house covered with wooden shingles the floor made from the knuckle-bones of deer. Delightful views of the gardens and particularly the Pinetum can be had by taking a trip on the 18 inch gauge railway.

Bicton Gardens are at East Budleigh 2½ miles north of Budleigh Salterton on A376. They are open daily in April and May from 2 to 6 p.m. and from June to September from 10 a.m. to 6 p.m.

Left: Delightful views of the Gardens and Pinetum can be had effortlessly from the miniature railway. *Below:* The Italian Garden is one of three separate areas at Bicton. The others are the American Garden and the Pinetum.

Knightshayes, a rich and growing collection

Knightshayes Court stands on a hillside overlooking the lovely valley of the River Exe. It is a site perfectly made for gardening, and successive generations have made good use of it for at least a hundred years. An avenue of large trees which sweeps up from the entrance gate once enclosed the path to the house, though now the drive takes another route. The broad terrace accommodating the house was no doubt cut out of the hillside in Victorian times and the series of intimate gardens enclosed in thick Yew hedges.

But it is during the last forty years that Knightshayes Court has acquired international fame for its rich and growing collection of exotic plants arranged with the utmost skill by Sir John and Lady Heathcote Amory. The slopes below the house have been enriched with fine trees, Rhododendrons and other shrubs, a large scree bed below the formal gardens provides ideal conditions for Gentians and choice alpine plants and the terrace itself has been richly planted, though one of the enclosed gardens remains, for contrast, almost completely unplanted, with only a circular pool and one white marble statue as ornament.

The main woodland garden, still in process of enlargement, lies beyond, laid out in long curving beds, built up where necessary with peat blocks and containing a vast collection of plants, including the tiny ones so often neglected in gardens of this magnitude. Among the Rhododendrons, Azaleas, Pieris, Magnolias, Daphnes, and other shrubs are Dog's Tooth Violets, Woodlilies, Hellebores, Hostas, Dicentras, Violets and many more.

To the west of the house a deep dell containing a pool has been surrounded by deciduous Azaleas, underplanted with Bluebells, a magnificent spectacle in spring.

Knightshayes lies 1½ miles north-east of Tiverton in Devon. Bus services run from Tiverton to Taunton and Minehead, and from Exeter to Minehead: alight at Bolham. The gardens are open to the public, in aid of various gardening charities, on Thursdays in April, May and June from 2–8 pm, and on the first Sunday in May and the last in June from 2–8 pm.

Left A series of intimate gardens enclosed by clipped Yew hedges surround the house. This is a corner of the rock garden. *Right* A water garden, unplanted for simplicity, houses a single statue. *Bottom right* Part of the garden in spring. *Over, Top left* A stone seat on one of the terraces. *Top right* The formal garden below the house contrasts well with the woodland planting. *Below* Part of the woodland garden in spring.

Montacute, relic of Elizabethan gardening

Montacute House was finished near the end of Queen Elizabeth I's reign. It is the most splendid and complete example of its kind remaining to us. The present garden bears little resemblance to the original for one reason: the present entrance side of the house was originally the back.

Near the entrance it is worth noticing two interesting trees. Both are specimens of the Monterey cypress *(Cupressus macrocarpa)*; one has been kept clipped as a piece of topiary, while the other has grown into a giant, probably the biggest specimen in Britain.

Against the north end of the house is a sunken lawn garden, bordered with formal evergreens, and at its centre a fountain. Designed by R. S. Balfour in 1894, its simple lines are very effective when looked down upon from the windows above. The balustrading and the obelisk finials surmounting it, so exactly match the similar features on the older walls that, with the passage of time, it is difficult to realise that they were made nearly three centuries later. By the south corner of the house, we ascend a broad flight of steps into a courtyard lying against the long and magnificent east front. At its corners are two exquisite pavilions, while the surrounding walls carry ornaments typical of the Elizabethan age, including two gazebos. There is no comparable piece of garden architecture still in existence. Now grassed over apart from a broad walk around it, and the walls most beautifully planted, the place is a gem, al-

Above: A pavilion overlooking the Courtyard Garden on the east side of the house.
Below: The Conservatory at the end of the terrace now houses ferns.

21

though it was originally the entrance court for the arrival and departure of carriages, rather than a garden.

Passing from it to the south side of the house, we find enclosed gardens, some of the yews in which are of considerable age.

A charming small nineteenth-century conservatory built in a Tudor style stands near the north corner. Within the house itself, can be seen sumptuous embroideries from Stoke Edith in Herefordshire, showing an entirely imaginary seventeenth-century garden.

Montacute, a National Trust property, is 4 miles west of Yeovil, on the north side of A3088. It is open from Easter Saturday to 30th September, from 11 a.m. to 6 p.m., daily except Tuesdays (the house is closed from 11.45 a.m. to 2 p.m.). From March to Easter and during October and November it is open on Wednesdays, Saturdays and Sundays, from 2–6 p.m. or dusk if earlier.

Above: Montacute, a back-to-front house, is an Elizabethan building.
Below: The northern sunken lawn garden has a formal lily pool and fountain.

Tintinhull, 20th Century formality

This Somerset garden, of no great size, but making use of modern ideas in planting, is a perfect example of early twentieth century simplicity and formality, with none of the over-elaborations, typical of Victorian days. The key is set by the eighteenth century West front of the house, built of almost golden-coloured stone, from the neighbouring Ham quarries. It is symmetrical on either side of a round-arched portico, from which descend steps to ground level. The main body of the garden is round either side of walk, leading from this door, and at right angles to the house. Steps drop down to a flagged terrace, with a low balustrade in front. Against the house stand benches

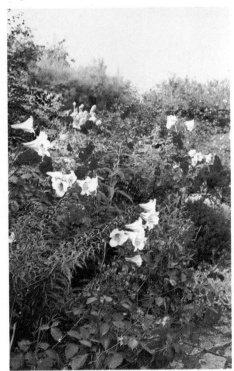

1 The water in a sparsely planted formal pool reflects light and shadow. Groups of waterlilies lead the eye to the distant pergola. 2 A formal paved area, relieved by ivy-leaved 'geraniums' planted in bold containers, leads on to the informal herbaceous border with an evergreen hedge background. 3 An attractive and highly fragrant combination of red roses and white regal lilies

and plant-filled tubs. From this terrace runs a paved walk, the flagstones laid in a simple geometrical pattern. It goes straight until it ends in a dense wall of clipped yews, which, however, gives the hint that it divides and passes to either side. Throughout its length are placed low cones of clipped box to emphasize the direct line as it goes through the small gardens that lie on either side. The first, the Eagle Court, is immediately below the house terrace and is a brick-walled, courtyard-like lawn, the path passing

The small, late seventeenth century manor house surrounded by a beautiful garden created by the late Mrs Reiss was donated by her to the National Trust in 1954. The public are admitted from April to October on Wednesday, Thursdays and Saturdays

out of it through a wide opening, on either side of which eagles surmount pillars.

Another smaller lawn with wider beds follows. From it shallow steps lead through an opening into a paved enclosure of yew, in the centre of which is a lily-pool. This terminates the main axis. Besides this long walk, there

are areas divided by clipped hedges and linked by low flights of steps, so giving interest to a flat site. One encloses a narrow, canal-like pool with a loggia at the end; in another stands a many-limbed cedar. Great use is made of plants in tubs and large ornamental pots, in a variety of shapes. Tintinhull House, a property of the National Trust, is 5 miles NW of Yeovil, a little S of A 303. The garden is open from April to October, on Wednesdays, Thursdays and Saturdays, and on Bank Holiday Mondays, from 2–6 p.m.

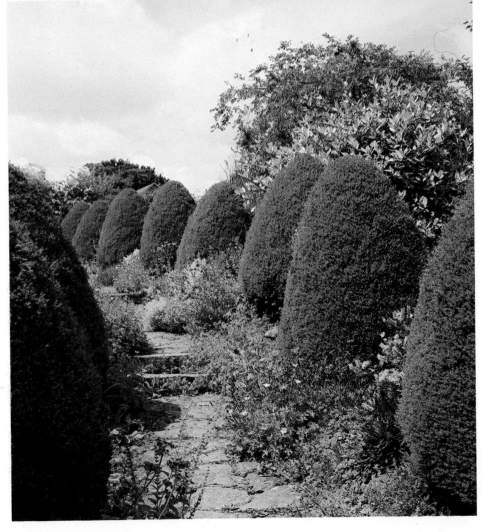

East Lambrook, a Manor in a Cottage Garden

East Lambrook Manor in Somerset is the home of Margery Fish, whose books on gardening are well known. The garden was made by Mrs Fish and her husband in 1937 round the fifteenth century house and sixteenth century malthouse. It has a friendly cottage atmosphere, with close and luxuriant planting.

Many rare and interesting plants are grown alongside old favourites, and the garden is a good example of natural gardening, which is popular today. Great use is made

Above, left: Fuchsias thrive in this garden and the walls provide protection for many climbers and other wall plants. *Above, right:* A large variegated sycamore dominates the lawn. *Below:* Clipped conifers form a miniature avenue. Plants sprawl along the pathway.

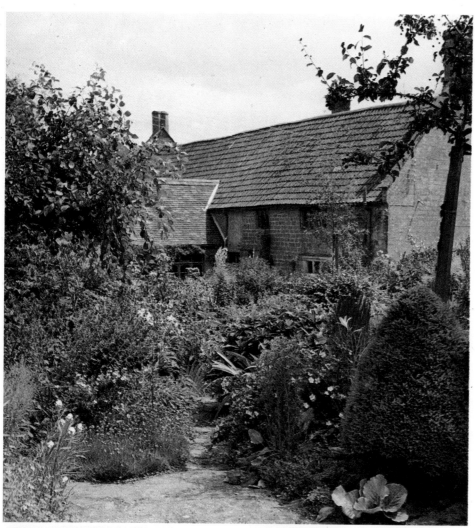

of the old walls, and foliage plays a big part in a scheme designed to be interesting at all seasons. A large variegated sycamore dominates the lawn at the back of the house, and the wide border under a high wall is always colourful. Clipped conifers and neat hedges contrast with the billowing silver foliage and branching euphorbias in the terraced garden beside the house.

There is a small silver garden facing south, and the old farm ditch, which originally separated two orchards, makes an unusual woodland garden. Here old primroses, hellebores and hardy geraniums grow under pollarded willows, while exotic plants, ornamental grasses and green flowers grow in another small garden.

East Lambrook is 3 miles north of A 303, between Ilchester and Ilminster. It is 9 miles from Yeovil and 18 from Taunton. The garden is open every Thursday in May, June, July and September from 2–5 p.m. and on some Sundays from 2–7 p.m.

East Lambrook Manor is a sophisticated cottage garden, where first-class varieties of plants, both old-fashioned and modern, are planted closely together in seeming confusion, yet their growth is carefully controlled.

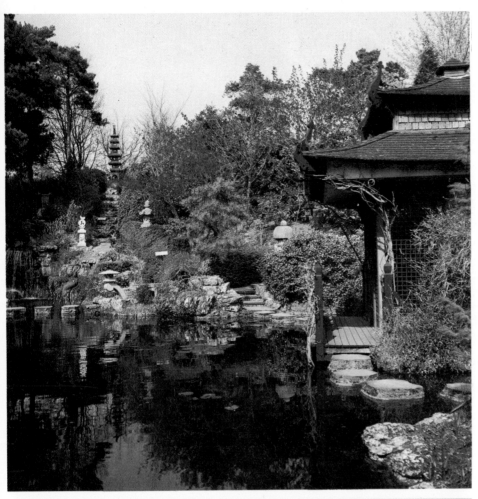

Compton Acres, a moorland conversion

The story of this series of gardens began just after the 1914–18 War, when the late T. W. Simpson, who had built a house on the site, began to convert what was largely moorland overlooking Poole Harbour into gardens of different styles. He spent £220,000 in landscaping, importing stone and rock, garden ornaments and plants. During the 2nd World War, the gardens deteriorated badly. They were restored by the next owner and opened to the public in 1952.

In 1964 the present owners, Mr and Mrs Brady, bought the estate and continue to open the gardens.

The Glen, Rock and Water Gardens contain a sub-tropical section with a chain of small lakes around which palms, mimosas, jacarandas, eucalyptus, bamboos and rhododendrons from the Himalayas grow. The path continues through a short tunnel to the rock garden. Here, rustic bridges cross the pools in which king carp swim among water lilies. From it can be seen the cascades which provide the water. Nearby is a viewpoint looking down the glen spread out below.

The Japanese Garden, surrounding an irregular pool, crossed by stepping stones, was built in the proper Japanese style, to the plans of a Japanese architect, using materials brought from Japan. Pagodas, carved lanterns, and figures, gateways—all full of symbolic meaning —abound. The plants, too, are Japanese.

As a contrast there is the garden built in the Roman manner from which, past herbaceous borders, the Italian Garden is reached. It is a large canal-like pool, its surroundings highly formal and decorated with urns and statues.

Finally, there is the Palm Court with more valuable statuary and a Wishing Well into which the visitor may throw money for charity.

The gardens are in Canford Cliffs Road, midway between Bournemouth and Poole. They are open daily from April to October—10.30 a.m. to 6.30 p.m. They close at dusk on Thursdays from June to August.

Above: Authentic material and statuary decorate the Japanese Garden. *Left:* The highly formal Italian Garden has a canal-like pool. *Over above:* Rustic bridges cross the pools of the Rock Garden. *Below:* Heaths of many kinds colour the Heather Dell.

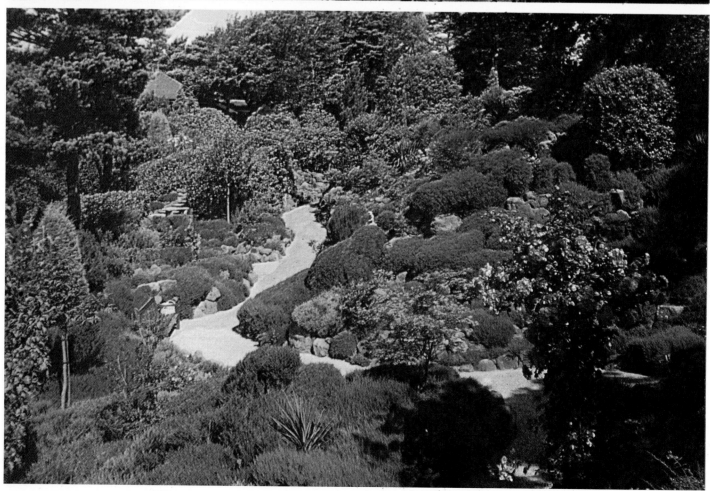

Athelhampton, formal and landscape gardening

Dorset abounds in fine Tudor houses and Athelhampton ranks with the best. It is fortunate that in the late nineteenth century it was given a garden which matches it so perfectly that it is difficult to realise it was made 300 years after the house was completed. This harmony is partly a matter of style, partly of material, a major part of the garden having been designed as a series of formal enclosures with pavilions, terraces and walls built of Ham stone similar to that used for the house. There are two quite large rectangular gardens and two smaller ones with a circle, or corona, in the centre from which each of the others can be reached. Long vistas have been preserved through these gardens both from north to south and from east to west but the full character and beauty of each can be seen only by entering it. There is much fine stone and iron work, several fountains and pools and a great deal of well-kept topiary, some grown to great size. One of the larger gardens is backed by a high stone terrace with flanking stone pavilions and from this some of the finest views of garden and house can be obtained.

The little River Piddle almost encircles Athelhampton and from the formal gardens a path leads beside the river to a very different series of gardens to the west of the house. Here the dominant

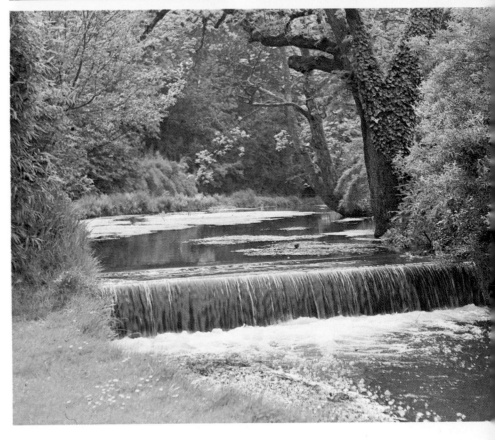

Top left Early summer at Athelhampton, with a profusion of Delphiniums and Paeonies. In the background is the ancient dovecote. *Centre* A secluded corner, the grass pathway flanked by white Shrub Roses and white Lilacs in full bloom. *Top right* One of the many long vistas through the gardens with statuary in the foreground. *Right* A waterfall and a riverside walk, the banks planted with water-loving plants and overhung by trees.

feature is an ancient dovecote standing in a large lawn and backed by a Yew alley which leads diagonally back to the river. Behind this alley are well-stocked herbaceous borders and the old reed-thatched stables. A little stream crosses the lawn and its banks are planted with moisture loving-plants with shrub Roses beyond. Development is continuing at the present time, especially in the improvement of the riverside garden.

Athelhampton is situated 1 mile east of Puddletown on A35. It is open on Wednesdays and Thursdays, from Easter to September and also on Bank Holiday Saturdays, Sundays and Mondays.

Above From this point, with its circular pool, radiate various walks to other parts of the garden. *Left* Some of the large topiary specimens with the Tudor building behind.

Stourhead, an informal Paradise garden

Stourhead was one of the first and still is one of the greatest landscape gardens in which the English threw off the fetters of Le Nôtre's French, rigid formality. Begun by the banker, Henry Hoare, after he inherited the property in 1741, the site was a bare, desolate valley with ponds in its bottom. The banks were planted with trees and the ponds were amalgamated and extended to make the present large lake. Around it a path was devised to provide a series of carefully contrived views, recalling the Italian landscapes, painted by Claude in the 17th-century, as well as incidents and events in classical authors such as Virgil.

The most important feature is the series of ornamental buildings, of the finest quality, most carefully contrived and placed (the architect Henry Flitcroft, whose principal work was Woburn Abbey, was closely concerned with these). These are no mere 'follies', but were full of significance to the Georgians, who were imbued with the classical spirit and had travelled the Grand Tour. There are temples, the Pantheon, the Temple of Flora and the Temple of Apollo, a fine grotto, a rock arch, a 'Gothick' cottage, wellheads and various bridges.

The subsequent history of the garden concerns its planting over the centuries with what were, at the time that they were put in, novelties. Many of these, particularly the conifers, are now outstanding specimens, while the massed plantings of rhododendrons and azaleas make a magnificent setting for the temples and other buildings, reflected as they are on a calm day of early summer in the lake. Later in the summer much colour is provided by hydrangeas, while in October the autumn colouring of the trees makes Stourhead well worth a visit.

Stourhead lies just off B3092 some nine miles south of Frome in Somerset, or, from Mere on the A303, a mile westward, then just over a mile northward on B3092.

The garden is open all the year, daily from 11 a.m. to 7 p.m., or dusk if earlier.

Above, the medieval Bristol High Cross at the entrance to the gardens. This was moved from Bristol to Stourhead in 1765; in the distance, across the lake, can be seen the Pantheon, the largest of the garden temples. *Top left*, the Palladian Bridge over an arm of the lake. *Left*, Stourhead in spring: the Rustic Cottage, with colourful rhododendrons in the foreground. *Over*, beside the lake stands the Pantheon, built in the mid-eighteenth century.

Sudeley, fine walks and views

Set in rolling Cotswold countryside in Gloucestershire, Sudeley Castle and garden recapture the order of a bygone age. The castle has been the scene of sad events and tumult, and was dismantled in Cromwellian times. In 1830 it passed to the Dent family, who planted the present garden and many of the trees and restored part of the castle. The ruins of mellowed Cotswold stone enhance the beauty of the trees and garden.

On entering the grounds one can see huge Walnut trees, at least one of which must be of great age. Beautifully clipped lines of Yews are an attractive feature of the garden. They shelter a formal flower garden planted within Box hedges. The garden is

said to be a replica of the medieval 'pleasaunce' with the original sundial, though the hedges are not much more than 100 years old. A fine Judas tree, a wonderful sight in May, grows beside the chapel.

Just beyond the entrance is a delightful pond, its surface covered with Water-lilies.

Around the pond margins ornamental trees have been planted with restraint. Particularly beautiful are the weeping Silver-leaved Pears, *Pyrus salicifolia* 'Pendula'.

Sudeley Castle lies half-a-mile south of Winchcombe on the A46 Cheltenham–Broadway road.

It is open every Wednesday and Thursday afternoon from May to September, Bank Holiday Sunday, Monday and Tuesday afternoons (not Christmas), alternate Sunday afternoons in May, June and July, and every Sunday afternoon in August and September. There are special Tuesday afternoon openings for booked coach parties.

Above Part of Sudeley Castle was restored after 1830, and the present garden laid out and many of the trees planted at that time. *Below left* A small fountain at the centre of the turved courtyard garden. *Below right* Near the entrance there is an attractive lily pool with stone balustrades surrounding it. The balustrades are a feature of the garden and are repeated in the background. Nearby is an aviary of rare birds. *Over* The great hedges of clipped Yew are a characteristic of the garden and shelter a formal garden planted with box hedges. The garden is thought to be a replica of the medieval 'pleasaunce'.

Westonbirt, a wooded wonderland

Westonbirt Arboretum, Gloucestershire, is not just a scientific collection of trees but an enchanting garden of ornamental woodland, interplanted with innumerable shrubs. At every season of the year it has interest for the visitor, ranging from the spectacular effect of the giant conifers, including some of the biggest in Britain, to the smaller trees and rare shrubs from all parts of the world.

In winter, for contrast, there are the brilliant red boles of the large Sequoias, the dazzling white bark of Birches and winter-flowering Cherries. From spring into summer, for unusual and often dazzling colour, there are the brilliant blossoms of Azaleas, Rhododendrons, Magnolias, and Cherries, and any

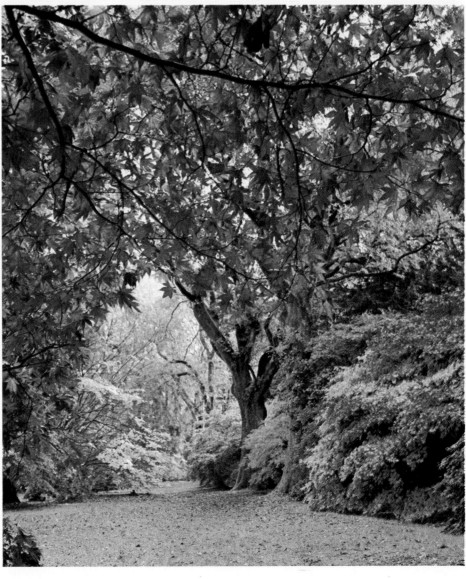

Above, left In autumn the bright tints of the fading leaves contrast brilliantly with the evergreens. *Above, right* A group of Libocedrus in the arboretum. *Below, right* Acer Glade, an area which is planted with Maples.

Above, left Birches and conifers in Silk Wood, where the trees can best be viewed by following the main path. *Above, right* Rhododendron blossoms in spring. *Below* The old and new Acer Glades are rich in autumn tints, and Maples also provide colour in other parts of the arboretum.

number of rarities, such as the Pyrenean Oak with its grey and gold catkins.

The most popular season is generally mid-October, when the old and the new glades of Maples are bathed in red and golden autumn tints.

Having soil that includes an area in which lime-hating plants such as Rhododendrons will thrive set among ground that suits the lime-lovers, the arboretum has a bigger variety of trees and shrubs than any tree collection in the British Isles and rarities are clearly labelled. When it was begun by Robert Holford in 1829, he laid out the ground in curving rides and broad, straight avenues so that all his trees were shown to their best effect. This policy has been followed by his successors with equal success and is now continued by the Forestry Commission, who took over the arboretum in 1956.

There are two distinct areas. On approaching the car park that to the immediate right, covering 116 acres, contains the more spectacular plantings such as the Maple

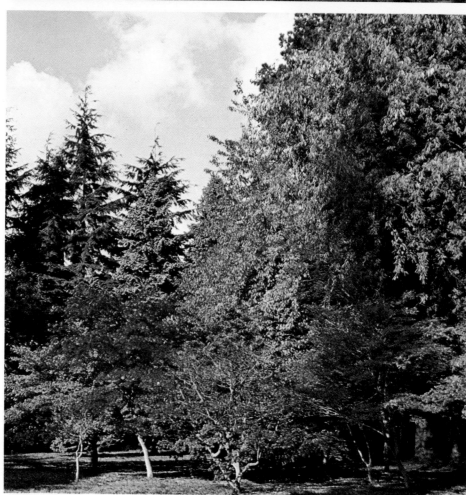

glades, while down a bank to the left, in Silk Wood, there are 45 acres of developed arboretum.

Westonbirt lies three miles south-west of Tetbury on the A433 road to Bath. It is open daily throughout the year, including Sundays, 10 am–8 pm (or sundown, if earlier). Admission is free, but a charge is made for parking.

Hidcote, unique in style and planting

Hidcote lies on the scarp of the Cotswolds between Stratford-on-Avon and Broadway with the Avon Vale spread out below.

The garden, which extends to about ten acres, is entirely the creation of an American, the late Major Lawrence Johnston, who acquired the place at the beginning of this century. It was a small bleak farmhouse with a solitary cedar in front of it and a clump of beech trees some yards away. On this unprom-

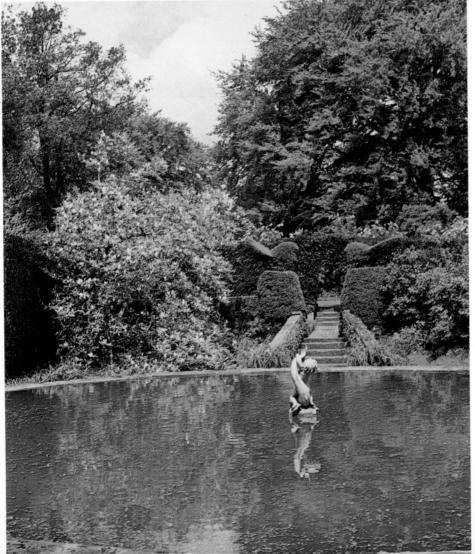

Above, looking along the double mixed borders to the Cedar of Lebanon. Dark-foliaged plants contrast with the roses. *Below*, the Bathing Pool Garden, surrounded by tall hedges, with topiary birds in the background.

ising site, using hedges for protection, Major Johnston made this garden which is now mature. Leading from the cedar, there is a straight central alleyway passing through a series of small compartment-like gardens, each one treated differently; one for example contains red-foliaged and red-flowered plants, another an alleyway which passes between twin gazebos and continues between hornbeams on trunks, the foliage closely clipped in the French manner; this is the Stilt Garden. In Mrs Winthrop's Garden, named after Major Johnston's mother, yellow predominates. A raised circular pool almost fills another small 'compartment'. The last compartment ends in a fine old gateway, through which is unexpectedly revealed a wide view over Shakespeare's country. In some of the tall, well-kept hedges several kinds of plants are used giving them a variegated appearance. These are often referred to as 'tapestry' hedges. In the Fuchsia Garden yew, box, holly, beech and hornbeam are used in the hedges, giving different textures and colours. There is a certain amount of topiary, mainly birds, but tall columns of yew dominate the Pillar Garden.

The other main feature is a wild garden. This follows a stream that meanders down the hill, along whose sides are planted many fine trees, flowering shrubs and moisture-loving plants to make a feature as informal as the compartment gardens are formal. These two axes are linked by further small gardens.

Elsewhere there are collections of old and species roses and clematis and a wide lawn sweeping up to the old beech tree. Throughout the garden there are fine examples of planting and good specimens of unusual plants.

The garden is now owned by the National Trust. It is at Hidcote Bartrim, three miles NE of Chipping Campden, one mile E of A46 and of B.4081. It is open from Easter Saturday until October 31st, daily except Tuesdays and Fridays, from 11 a.m. until 8 p.m.

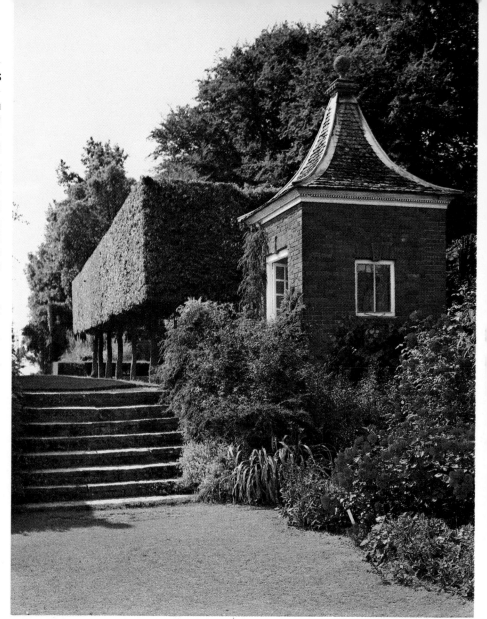

Above, part of the double mixed border leading to the twin garden houses or gazebos, of which one is shown. Beyond is part of the Stilt Garden, remarkable for the closely clipped hornbeams grown on short straight trunks. *Below*, part of the Pillar Garden dominated by topiary columns in clipped yew.

Harold Peto at Buscot Park

Buscot Park, Berkshire, is a fine example of the work of Harold Ainsworth Peto, who continued the work of William Robinson and Gertrude Jekyll in breaking away from the stuffy, over-formal style of Victorian gardening.

Peto was one of the foremost garden designers, who developed a new style of simplified classical naturalness and understood the art of planting as well as design. It was William Robinson and Gertrude Jekyll who by their example and writings brought informal gardening with herbaceous borders and naturalised plants back into vogue.

In 1787, Buscot Park was merely a 'modern' house on a hill top with a 'pretty piece of water'.

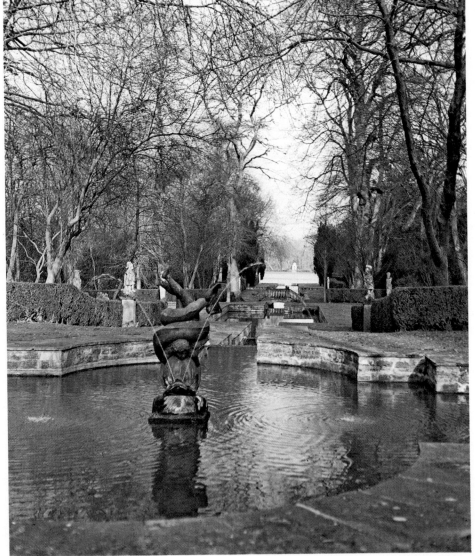

Above, left A formal pool at Buscot Park, Berkshire, with the lake created by 'Capability' Brown in the distance. *Above, right* The house in its simple setting. *Right* The fountain at the top of the canal walk which leads down in a series of levels to the 20-acre lake below.

Peto, who lived from 1854 to 1933, showed his genius in using the lake to make a fine water garden. The principal feature which he created is a long grass walk with a narrow canal at its centre between high trees falling in a series of stages towards the lake. The lake presents a breath-taking vista as it suddenly appears in view.

The walk by the canal is full of varied interest. At one stage there is a fountain, and at another the canal is crossed by a bridge. The canal is planted with Water-lilies and at the main intersection there are fine vistas crossing the main one.

Later additions to Peto's work include a young avenue of Cypress Oaks and a group of figures—examples of modern sculpture.

Buscot Park is a National Trust property and lies three miles north-west of Faringdon on the A417 Lechlade–Faringdon road. It is open from April to September on Wednesdays and the first week-end (Saturdays and Sundays) in each of these months, 2–6 pm. It is also open between October and March on Wednesdays, 2–6 pm.

Above Fine vistas cross the main one which runs the length of the canal, and are framed by well-sited trees. The eye is caught at intervals by such views. *Below* The courtyard pool.

Water and woodlands at Windsor

The Savill Garden was started in 1932 as a water and bog garden around one of the smaller ponds in Windsor Great Park, Berkshire. Since the garden was started it has steadily grown, and now covers over 20 acres. It includes many plants popular with modern gardeners. There are some particularly fine herbaceous borders, as well as Rose gardens, raised beds for rock plants, shrub borders and climbers. Although it lacks the architectural interest of a fine house, the Savill garden is nevertheless of great interest and was created by Sir Eric Savill, deputy ranger of Windsor Great Park.

For instance, a wild woodland garden of great beauty has been made in the outlying parts of the garden, and further gardens have been added to the south in the direction of Virginia Water, the largest of the lakes in the park. The original bog garden now includes another large pond specially dug to show the interest of this type of garden. A wall built of old brick provides support for climbing plants. Further features of the park include the Punch Bowl, a natural amphitheatre filled with evergreen Azaleas and Japanese Maples, a Heather garden, a valley of deciduous Azaleas and the Valley Garden, beautifully landscaped.

The Savill Garden, which is Crown property, is reached from Wick Lane via Englefield Green from the A30 road. The garden is open daily from March to October between 10 am and 6 pm.

Below The Savill Garden in Windsor Great Park is a water and bog garden built around a lake. *Above top* The Heather Garden is in a valley. *Right* The flowering Cherries in spring are a delightful feature of the garden. *Below right* The natural beauty of the site has been enhanced. *Over, top left* A spring scene in the garden. *Top right* The Azaleas in the Punch Bowl in May. *Below* The woodland forms the background to the Azaleas and shrubs.

Cliveden, quiet country retreat by the river

A wide and famous view of the River Thames flowing between steep, wooded slopes seen over an immense lawn lingers in the mind's eye after a visit to the famous house and gardens at Cliveden, Buckinghamshire. The diarist, John Evelyn, described it in 1679: . . .'tis a romantic object, and the place altogether answers the most poetical description that can be made . . . on the platform is a circular view to the utmost verge of the horizon,

Above Magnolia and Cherry trees and the old Canning Oak, in the spring. The Cliveden reach of the Thames can be seen beyond, as the estate enjoys a unique position on high ground above the river. *Right* The pagoda, used in the Great Exhibition of 1851, makes a focal point in the Japanese Garden.

Above The south front and terrace, which was constructed in 1666, overlooking an old parterre. A wealth of tree planting is to be seen at Cliveden. *Right* A fountain with central statuary in glistening white, stands at the end of the wide grass-flanked drive, at the northern approach to the house.

which with the serpenting of the Thames is admirably surprising.'

This view is enjoyed from the dominating architectural feature at Cliveden, the great red brick terrace built by William Winde in 1666. Upon it now stands a handsome Victorian building. An array of shrubs and climbers are trained against the terrace and at its base is a wide, well-planted border. The view is enhanced by grey Atlas Cedars flanking the lawn and Box-edged parterres of original design. Beside the lawn a delightful path winds down to the riverside.

Elsewhere there is much worth seeing, including the eighteenth-century temples by Giacomo Leoni, who helped to introduce the Palladian architectural movement in Britain. A Japanese-style garden surrounds a temple-like building surmounted by a weird, fish-like figure of a monster. The garden has matured Japanese Maples, Bamboos and other shrubs. A wide, grass avenue has

as its focal point a glistening white, ornate fountain. There is also a water garden with a good selection of Water-lilies. The shrubberies are interesting.

Cliveden is 2 miles north of Taplow on the B476 road to Hedsor. The road forms the northern boundary to the grounds, the entrance being at Hedsor lodge at the north end. Opening times for summer, roughly April to October, are for the garden: Wednesdays, Thursdays, Fridays, Saturdays, Sundays and Bank Holidays, 11 am–6.30 pm; house: Wednesdays, Saturdays and Sundays, 2.30–5.30 pm.

Ascott, terraces, turf and topiary

Though set in typical English countryside with wide views sweeping over the Vale of Aylesbury, Ascott is not a typically English garden; it is more representative of the nineteenth-century Continental style.

The ground is terraced so that the view is unobstructed. On one terrace, called the Madeira Walk, the shelter is used to protect tender plants. On the lawns around the house we first notice a feature of the place—the presence of many variegated and coloured-leaved forms of trees and shrubs. And from this upper level we observe too the clever and extensive use of clipped evergreens to form compartments. One that is looked down from above has at its centre a rather baroque fountain set simply in the grass.

Elsewhere is a remarkable garden in the nineteenth-century French style. From a small pond of geometric design surrounded by

a gay parterre rises, from a base of dolphins, their tails entwined, a fountain that epitomises the last century.

Around it is topiary cut into cork-screws and other odd shapes. Another remarkable example of topiary will also be noticed—a sundial, spread out on a lawn, whose gnomon and hours are all cut from living evergreens.

On the other side of the house is an informal Lily pool with its borders well-planted with trees and shrubs in a typically English manner.

In spring there is colour from many Japanese Cherries and massed bulbs that are naturalised.

Ascott is a National Trust property lying ½ mile east of Wing, 2 miles south-west of Leighton Buzzard on the south side of A418. Opening times vary from year to year.

Right above A formal garden in the nineteenth-century French style, with a sundial and dolphin fountain behind. *Right* The house, built in the Tudor style, stands above the terraces with an open view towards Ivinghoe Beacon, Herts.
Below left The summer house is approached along a gravel walk bordered by colourful borders, always filled with seasonal planting.
Below right A feature of the whole garden at Ascott is the colour contrasts in the trees and shrubs and there are many clipped evergreens. *Over* The lead fountain is surrounded by a clipped Golden Yew hedge and well-kept circular lawn.

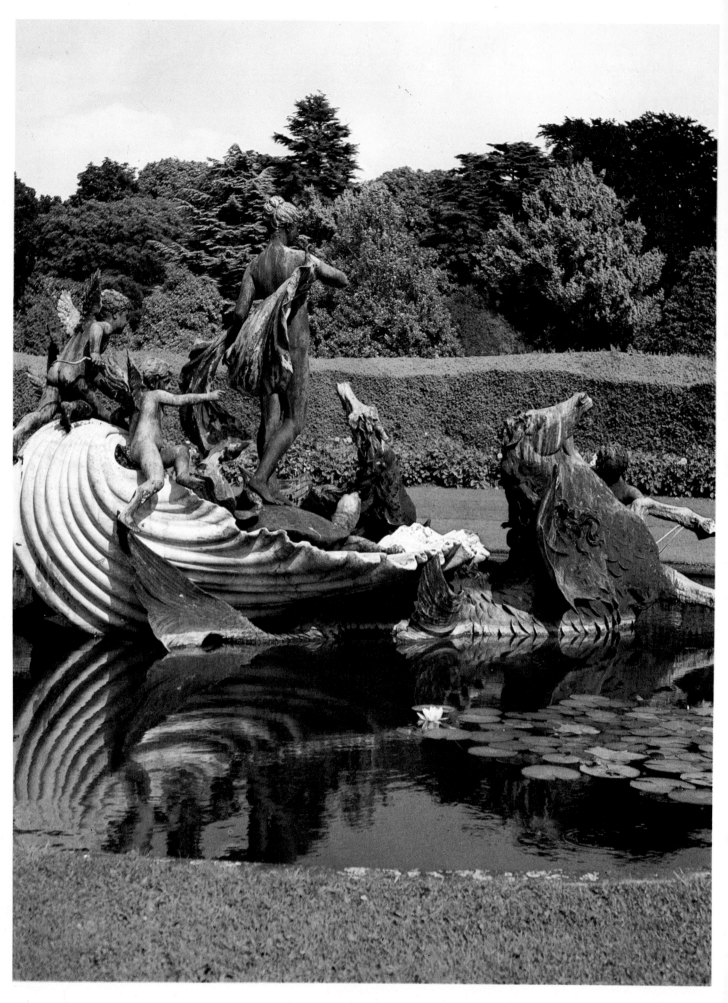

Eighteenth-century Stowe still inspires

From the early years of the eighteenth century English garden makers were searching for a new style, less formal than the French, Italian and Dutch gardens then fashionable, and corresponding more closely to a romantic conception of nature. One of the leaders of the movement was William Kent. Stowe, Buckinghamshire, was his greatest creation. At Stowe, Kent worked with Charles Bridgeman, a formalist, from whom Kent eventually took over the designing of the garden. Kent developed to the full his ideas for a series of garden landscapes, each conceived as a picture much as an artist might conceive it. This was a period when dilettante interest in classical buildings was at its height, and Kent adorned his landscapes with temples, columns, statues and bridges in the classical manner. He swept away flower beds, parterres and formal pools, replacing them with grass following the natural contours of the land, with groups and belts of trees to open up the loveliest vistas and views of artificial lakes so cunningly formed that they appeared entirely natural.

Lancelot ('Capability') Brown, who was later to design so many English gardens, worked at Stowe under Kent. Many of the eighteenth-century landscape gardens were later destroyed or greatly altered, but Stowe has remained largely untouched apart from the necessary replacement of trees.

Today Stowe is a great public school and its grounds must accommodate new buildings, playing fields, a golf course and facilities for sailing and rowing, but most of these do not noticeably detract from Kent's great design which remains as inspiring and as beautiful as ever.

Stowe is about three miles north of Buckingham. The gardens are open to the public in the afternoons from 2 pm to 6.30 pm at Easter and for a fortnight about the end of July.

Below, left The gothic temple, begun before 1744, built to an eccentric triangular plan, is an early 'gothic-revival' building. *Below, right* The Cobham monument (about 1750), 115 feet high, has been repaired in recent years. *Over, above* One approach to Stowe is by the Oxford Avenue, over the Oxford Bridge and between the Boycott pavilions (about 1728). *Below* The Palladian Bridge (about 1744).

Ashridge, a garden in the Chilterns

A community has existed at Ashridge, Hertfordshire, since the thirteenth century when it was a monastery. After the dissolution of the monasteries, it became a royal residence. The present building dates from 1815 and to the south of it there is a level garden with numerous interesting features.

Humphry Repton carried out much work at Ashridge and is reputed to have made seventeen smaller gardens within the whole to break up the rather level overall effect. A few of these gardens remain. There is, for instance, the Monks' Garden, which consists of a parterre surrounding a cast iron monument (recently restored). The Monks' Barn runs along one side of this garden and is divided from it by a herbaceous border. There is too, a circular Rose garden surrounded by a high hedge, and also a small garden with Wisterias trained as standards in front of a conservatory. The orangery has now become an integral part of the building and forms a perfect background for the small Italian garden with central fountain and fish pool. The massed planting of Rhododendrons lends colour across the lawn.

A unique feature of the garden is an immense square skating pond formerly flooded in winter, now with steps leading down to the paved base. Two tree-houses or arbours nearby are unusual. The fernery and grotto made of Hertfordshire pudding stone were added in the nineteenth century and the tunnel beyond may well have been an old ice house. To

Above The grey stone buildings of Ashridge House are in contrast to the local flint, which is still to be seen in some churches and older buildings. *Below* The garden includes fine plantings of trees and shrubs. *Over, top* The conservatory. *Below, left* The terrace close to the house is treated formally with clipped Yews and small, Box-edged beds. *Below, right* The Monks' Garden was designed by Humphry Repton, who carried out much work at Ashridge. This garden is next to the old cloisters of the Monks' Barn and forms a secluded and peaceful part of the main garden.

the west an avenue of Liquidambar trees planted in 1936 leads along the extremity of the garden to a hard-to-find Bible Garden—containing a small stone carving of an open Bible.

Amid the grounds of the extensive Ashridge Park administered by the National Trust, the garden itself is owned by the Ashridge Managements Committee, the building being used as a college. It is situated on an escarpment in the Chiltern Hills, 4 miles north of Berkhamsted, and can be approached by a toll road from either Berkhamsted or Little Gaddesden.

The gardens are open on Saturdays and Sundays and Bank Holiday Mondays from April to September inclusive, from 2 pm—6 pm.

Hampton Court, garden of a jealous king

The garden of this palace was the first in Britain to be made in the magnificent style of the Renaissance. Cardinal Wolsey began it in 1514, with sheltered alley-ways, elaborate knots and fountains. The jealous Henry VIII acquired it in 1529 and greatly enlarged and elaborated it. He built a magnificent mount, or viewpoint, on a foundation of a quarter of a million bricks, surmounted by a magnificent arbour, laid out flower beds surrounded by painted rails and erected effigies of heraldic beasts. None of this remains, but pictures of it are in the palace. There is a small knot garden planted in 1924, to give an idea of what it was like at the time. E.R. and the date 1568 was carved on the bay window overlooking it.

Much more remains of the next phase of the garden which was designed by London and Wise for William III and Mary at the time of Wren's additions. This is the great Fountain Garden with its avenues radiating from the magnificent portico at the centre of the east front. It is now greatly changed; there were originally several more fountains and in what is now grass was an intricate network of flower beds, or parterre.

Another relic of this period is the maze near the lion gate. This was at one corner of an area of trees and shrubs intersected by paths winding in and out, called The Wilderness. Nearby is the tilt yard the scene of tournaments in the time of Henry VIII which has now been turned into a modern garden.

To the south of Wren's building lies the large Privy Garden laid out formally with paths, lawns and trees and decorated with statuary and a fountain. This, too, was much more ornate with scroll-like flower beds in the days of William and Mary. On either side the ground is raised. That on the west is an alleyway of wych elms called Queen Mary's Bower. By the foot of the steps leading

1 A view of the Canal or 'Long Water'. 2 The Knot Garden was planned and restored in 1924 as an example of a garden of the 16th century. 3 Henry VIII's Pond or Sunken Garden looking across to the Banqueting House

to it is a gateway passing a series of small flower gardens enclosed within brick walls known as the Tudor Garden. Hampton Court Palace lies on the North bank of the Thames not far from Kingston. It is easily reached by rail from Waterloo or by Greenline bus. It is well signposted and motorists can approach it by turning off the A3 at the Scilly Isles roundabout near Esher, or by crossing Kingston Bridge and turning left.

The Palace and Gardens are open all the year; from May to September on weekdays (9.30 a.m. to 6.00 p.m.) and on Sundays (2.00 p.m. to 4.00 p.m.); from November to February on weekdays (9.30 a.m. to 4.00 p.m.) and on Sundays (2.00 p.m. to 4.00 p.m.); in March, April and October on weekdays (9.30 a.m. to 5.00 p.m.) and on Sundays (2.00 p.m. to 5.00 p.m.). They are not open Good Friday, Christmas Day or Boxing Day.

1 Henry VIII's Pond or Sunken Garden is planted up each spring and autumn. 2 The 17th century garden was replanned and restored in period style

A colourful choice of trees at Winkworth

The site of this fine tree collection in Surrey, made entirely in the present century, could hardly be bettered on a hillside curling around a large lake. Surrounded by sheltering plantations of native trees and conifers with Bluebells each spring, the arboretum has been steadily extended over the years and planting continues at the present time. Though the arboretum is not formal in design, there is a pleasant diversity in the planting, some of the trees and shrubs being placed as isolated specimens, some in groups, yet others in dense plantations with wonderful autumn colour. Paths of grass or beaten soil lead down from the car park at the top of the hillside to the lower level, through a glade of Azaleas which are at their best in May and a

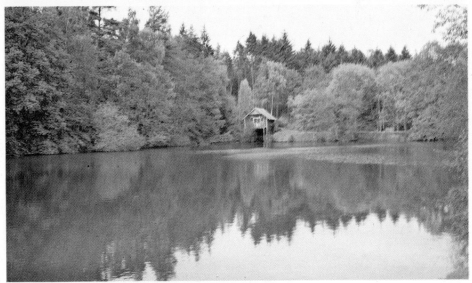

Top Some of the wide variety of Maples. *Below* Looking across the lake at Winkworth. *Over, above* Winkworth Arboretum is worth visiting at any time of the year, but is particularly beautiful at Bluebell time. *Below* Japanese Maples, Azaleas and, behind, Larches, Douglas Firs and other Conifers.

wider path follows roughly the line of the lake. There are long vistas through the trees and more open glades, but the finest comprehensive view of the arboretum is to be obtained from the far side of the lake, where there is also a car park and an alternative approach.

Cedars and Blue Spruces are particularly well placed, there is a fine collection of Mountain Ash, or Sorbus, and a great many Maples and Sumachs for brilliant autumn leaf. Cotoneasters produce berries freely and continue their display far into the winter. Hydrangeas for late summer colour are also a feature at Winkworth; indeed this is an arboretum which can be visited with pleasure at any time of the year.

Winkworth, owned by the National Trust, is about two miles south of Godalming. It is open through the hours of daylight throughout the year.

Polesden Lacey, gardening on chalk

This Regency house stands on a chalk ridge with wide views over undulating, park-like Surrey countryside and is surrounded by wide lawns and groups of trees. Its oldest and most distinguished feature is a terraced walk backed by aged trees with a view towards Ranmore Common. This walk was greatly extended by the dramatist R. B. Sheridan and bears his name.

Around the house the more or less formal lay-out is typical of the early decades of this century, consisting of a number of distinct but connected areas form-

Above The Regency house, now the property of the National Trust stands on high ground and commands wide views over the surrounding Surrey hills. *Below* A formal paved path with Rose pergola is guarded by heraldic beasts at the wrought-iron gate.

ing an extension to the house. One is a Rose Garden within old brick and flint walls, against which climbers are trained; another feature is a short avenue of the erect-growing Japanese Cherry Ama-no-gawa. Other small gardens are surrounded by clipped Yew or Box hedges.

Below these is a bank descending to the extensive lawn. On this sharp slope are many shrubs, including a remarkable mass of the low, spreading Knap Hill or Pfitzer Juniper *(Juniperus media pfitzeriana)*. There are many fine trees on the lawn, including some tall, slender, Grey Spruces *(Picea pungens glauca)*, and notable Beeches. There is also an open-air theatre.

Polesden Lacey is a National Trust property. The grounds are open daily all the year from 11 am to dusk. It is 2½ miles south of Bookham station and 3 miles west of Dorking. It is reached from A426 by a road running south from Great Bookham.

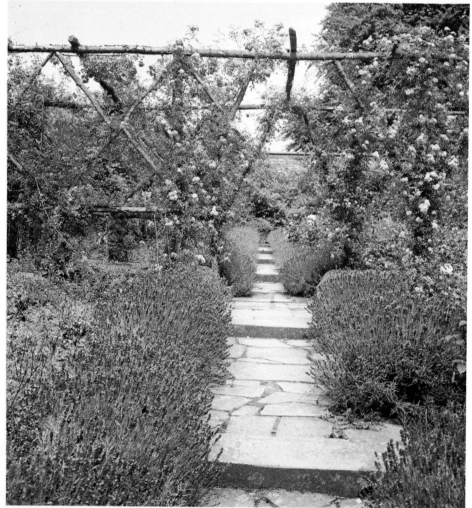

Above Prunus 'Ama-no-gawa' is used effectively in this formal avenue. *Below* On an estate famous for its trees, it is refreshing to find the cottage garden atmosphere among these roses.

World-famous Kew Gardens

The Royal Botanic Gardens, Kew, Surrey, covering an area of 300 acres on the south side of the River Thames, are the home of one of the largest botanical collections of plants in the world. A garden for a botanical collection was started over 200 years ago by Princess Augusta, widow of the Prince of Wales. With the help of John Stuart, the Earl of Bute, she began the garden in the grounds of her home at Kew House. The garden of neighbouring Richmond House was later linked with Kew House garden, and the whole property taken over by the nation in 1841.

Sir William Chambers (1723–96), the British architect, designed a fine orangery and was also

Above The Queen's Garden is a reconstruction of a seventeenth-century garden. *Below, left* A Rhododendron walk in early summer. *Below, right* The palm house. *Over, above* An oriental temple seen in a perfect setting among Azaleas. *Below, left* The temperate house, which contains a remarkable and large collection of plants. *Below, right* The Chinese-style pagoda, designed by Sir William Chambers in the eighteenth century, is one of the more famous and eccentric features of Kew Gardens.

responsible for the fantastic pagoda built in the Chinese style.

There is interest all the year round at Kew, and even in winter, or on a day of unpleasant weather, it is well worth visiting the fernery and conservatory and cactus,

orchid and alpine houses near the main gate. The famous rock garden is also in this part of the gardens. Near the Victoria Gate stands the 120-year-old palm house, the most beautiful building incorporating glass in its construction in Britain. In spring the Rhododendron dell and nearby Azalea and Magnolia gardens are most delightful, with a fine view across the river to Syon House, seat of the Duke of Northumberland.

From this part of the garden an avenue of Oaks leads to the palm house and lake, and from the pagoda you can reach the large temperate house, and the greenhouse containing a collection of Australian plants.

These are some of the main features, but everywhere there is something of beauty or interest for the visitor, not excepting the new historical garden by Kew Palace.

Kew Gardens are 1 mile from Richmond and approached from London by bus, Underground service, or, in summer, by boat. They open every day (excepting Christmas Day) from 10 am to 8 pm in summer, and from 10 am to sunset in winter.

Wisley, a garden for all gardeners

In 1878 G. F. Wilson, an amateur gardener, bought an estate of derelict woodland at Wisley in Surrey. He opened clearings, made paths and ponds, and naturalised rhododendrons, lilies, irises and many other plants. After his death in 1902 this pioneer woodland garden was given in trust to the Royal Horticultural Society. Now extended to some 150 acres, practically every kind of gardening, ornamental and utilitarian, possible in Britain is displayed and studied. Near the entrance are the labora-

1 A stream meanders through the rock garden ablaze with spring colour. 2 The azalea dell near Battleston Hill in May. 3 A view of the alpine meadow and rock garden from the wild garden. Primulas and bog plants flourish by the stream

tories against whose sheltered walls tender plants are grown. Nearby are lawns with seasonally planted beds. Ahead is the range of glass houses, running due west, sheltering plants that range from the barely tender to tropical orchids.

To their south lie the mixed borders where shrubs and other plants are grown together in a practical arrangement. During the summer, the rose garden westward of this should be visited; through this are the fruit gardens.

Particularly in spring and early summer the wide grass path through the mixed borders should be followed up hill. It passes through massed azaleas and rhododendrons. To its left lies Battlestone Hill with paths winding among camellias, rhododendrons and similar shrubs. To the right of the broad walk are ornamental cherries.

The alpine meadow (with masses of tiny daffodils in spring), the world famous rock garden and the wild garden are reached by proceeding due west along the line of glass houses. From the wild garden the heath garden lies to the north-west. This merges with Seven Acres, a spacious planting of trees and shrubs around a large pool.

The long herbaceous borders (with the trials gardens on their left) are seen half-right from the laboratory. At their end Seven Acres lies to the left and the large pinetum—a collection of conifers —to the right. Through this is

A view of the Royal Horticultural Society's wild garden at Wisley in Surrey. In such a natural labour-saving setting, many plants such as primulas, lilies and ferns flourish.

Howard's Field, an example of planting on extremely dry, sandy soil that cannot be watered.

The gardens are open daily to the public except Good Friday and Christmas from 10 a.m. to 7.30 p.m. or sunset if earlier, and on Sundays, when admission is restricted to holders of Fellow's tickets. They lie on the north-west just off A3 between Ripley and Cobham, 20 miles from London. Green Line Coach 715 runs within 5 minutes walk, taking about 1 hour 20 minutes from London. Enquire times from London Transport Executive. Restaurant and free car park.

Sheffield Park, the glory of autumn

Unlike most gardens (Westonbirt Arboretum is another) Sheffield Park was designed with the knowledge that we often have glorious days in October and that by planting many trees and shrubs, comparatively recently introduced, the brilliance of autumn colour of thrilling intensity can extend the gardener's pleasures far into the autumn. In spring, the ground sheeted with bluebells, the gardens are equally enjoyable.

The garden as we now see it was the work of A. G. Soames. It was begun in 1909. His site was a series of five lakes in a descending chain, a 'Capability' Brown landscape with which Humphry Repton had been concerned. Around them Soames planted, usually in large numbers, trees and shrubs, often used only as single specimens, to give a series of carefully composed pictures and colour-schemes. Sometimes these are pale, the colours provided by giant bushes of rhododendrons, the Angelo hybrids, raised by Soames himself.

These are followed by the heavily-scented, large-flowered white and pink Loderi rhododendrons, raised at Leonardslee. At a later season the blue of massed gentians is a famous sight. The full glory of blazing colour is left for autumn, when among the rich greens of spiring conifers—a number of them rare—every shade of crim-

Massed plantings of many-coloured rhododendrons, seen across a water-lily studded lake. Tall conifers give contrast of shape.

son, red, gold and yellow, particularly from massed plantings of the North American Tupelo tree, *(Nyssa sylvatica)* is reflected in the lakes.

Sheffield Park Gardens lie midway between East Grinstead and Lewes, East of A275, 5 miles north-west of Uckfield. They are open from March 30th to October 31st: during April on Wednesdays, Saturdays and Sundays, from 2-7 p.m.; from May to September, daily from 11 a.m. to 7 p.m.; during October, daily from 12 noon until 5 p.m.

They are also open on Easter, Spring and Late Summer Bank Holiday Mondays from 12 noon until 7 p.m., and during November by arrangement with the Head Gardener.

Contrasts of spring and autumn at Sheffield Park. *Above:* rhododendrons, water-side irises and trees grown for their coloured foliage contrast with the sombre hues of the conifers. *Below:* the fiery leaves of maples and *Nyssa sylvatica* light up the autumn scene.

Tender plants thrive at Wakehurst

Wakehurst Place, near Ardingly, Sussex, is an Elizabethan mansion built of local sandstone. It is situated on a narrow ridge of land with deep valleys to the west and east, which drain away much of the cold air when radiation frosts occur early in spring. Because of this it has been possible to grow many plants in the garden that would normally be considered too tender for this part of Britain. A truly magnificent collection has been built up in the past 60 years or so.

Much of the planting in the upper part of the garden follows the familiar glade style, with beds of irregular size and shape permanently planted with trees and shrubs, and separated by areas of mown grass. There is also an extensive heath garden in which the Heathers are pleasantly and naturally associated with other shrubs, including Brooms, which survive on acid soils and with a close covering of other plants.

There are several large lakes, the one nearest to the house being flanked by an exceptionally large and well-planted rock garden, in which Japanese Maples are a feature. Rhododendrons also encircle this rock garden and a path leads on past fine plantations of Hydrangeas, Magnolias and Azaleas. The path then continues past more lakes and down through Rhododendron woods to the Ardingly brook. Up the brook valley the more energetic visitor can return by a more circuitous route.

There is also an extensive pinetum on the high ground beyond the Heather garden in which grows the lovely Mexican *Pinus patula* with slender drooping needles. The Sikkim Larch, with hanging branchlets, and *Picea*

Above top Some of the magnificent Rhododendrons, Camellias, Acers, Conifers and broad-leaved trees, for which Wakehurst Place is famous. *Above* A woodland glade, in which, after the blaze of the Rhododendrons has died away, much quiet colour is provided by the infinite greens of the tree foliage. *Left* A few of the many Acers. *Over* Autumn at Wakehurst Place can be one of the most colourful times of the year.

breweriana, Brewer's Weeping Spruce, also grow there. The gardens, now belonging to the National Trust, are used as an extension of the Royal Botanic Gardens, Kew.

Wakehurst is 1½ miles north-west of Ardingly on the B2028 road. It is open all the year round (except Christmas Day) at varying times during the afternoon.

Borde Hill, connoisseurs' choice

Borde Hill is a delightful stone-built Sussex manor house standing on a low saddle of ground a little to the north of Haywards Heath. The original garden is in the landscape style with a large lawn to the south terminated by a deep ha-ha (see Ha-ha), permitting uninterrupted views towards the South Downs and, to the north, an entrance drive with a little terraced garden below it, which equally effectively displays the rolling, well-wooded countryside in that direction. The southern vista is flanked by trees which extend to form a woodland where the ground rises and then falls into two large dells, perhaps the sites of medieval mining operations.

Into this lovely setting a notable collection of choice plants has been introduced during the present century. Rhododendrons fill the formal beds in the terrace garden beside the drive and flank the path leading to the woodland. They also fill large parts of the woodland itself and the bigger of the two dells, in the shelter of which they have grown very large. Great drifts of highly-coloured Azaleas ring the main lawn and grow on the lower slopes of the woodland. At its highest point, where there is another smaller house with a little garden of its own, half-hidden in the trees and bushes, there are raised stone-edged beds and a somewhat formal design, though the whole is so heavily clothed with Anthemis and other hardy plants that its formal character is almost concealed.

The second of the two dells has been developed as a water and bog garden. Here will be found the Ostrich Plume and other hardy ferns together with Hostas, Irises, Astilbes, Euphorbias, Ligularias and many more plants with fine foliage to supplement their flowers.

The garden is reached on the Balcombe road over 1 mile north of Haywards Heath. Opening times are Sundays and Wednesdays, April to August, 2 to 7 pm, and Sundays in September from 2 to 5 pm.

Left, below Borde Hill is a garden where the connoisseur will find many collections of interesting plants. Here, Heathers cover the ground beneath Pine trees. *Left, bottom* A statue by the Italian sculptor Antonio Tantardini of a veiled woman. *Below* Azaleas are quite a feature of the garden and the 'Azalea Ring' is outstandingly lovely in May. *Over, above* The manor house stands in beautiful surroundings. *Over, below* Near the walled garden, where there are examples of Camellias 'Donation' and 'Salutation', there is some fine topiary work.

Nymans, a garden round a ruined house

The gardens at Nymans, Sussex, are best described as a blend of formal and informal in which the trees, shrubs and plants—always of fine quality—and their arrangement, play a predominant part. The garden, on well-drained, fertile sandy loam was begun by Mr Ludwig Messel eighty years ago. His friends, the famous gardeners William Robinson and Gertrude Jekyll

1 A view of Nymans a National Trust property. The garden was laid out 70 to 80 years ago by Ludwig Messel in collaboration with some of the best gardeners of his day such as William Robinson and Gertrude Jekyll. 2 Nymans is famous for its rhododendrons and camellias.

advised and encouraged him on its development. It is a garden to-day, with a surprising feature: the house which it surrounded is largely a burned-out shell—a true ruin of grey stone, rather than those of the artificial kind such as the follies of the eighteenth century. Strangely, the fire did little damage to the tender plants that were sheltered by the walls of the building; they can now ramble inside the glassless windows.

Around the house on one side are the lawns, with banks of flowering shrubs, and on the other, a walled garden with an Italian fountain, at its centre, with topiary around it. A heather garden, one of the first in the country, a rose garden and

The stone used to construct the grey calcined walls of the house and features such as the dovecote, shown here, has weathered attractively and blends with the trees and shrubs for which Nymans is famous.

a pinetum are among the other pleasant parts of the garden, in which originated that fine shrub, *Eucryphia* 'Nymansay'. This last, indeed, with its large white flowers, with golden centres in late summer, is freely planted among the sombre conifers in the pinetum. In an area curiously called a reserve garden, under Scots pines, the Chinese rhododendrons such as the huge-leaved *R. sinogrande* flourish. Past them a glade is designed to display the autumn colours of foliage and berries—

enkianthus, pyracantha, *Rosa moyesii* and the Chinese Maples. Here, too, is the dense carpet of spring-flowering dwarf rhododendrons from the mountains of western China. Beyond is an area of exceptional interest called Tasmania, in which grow plants from that country and the Andes.

The gardens, now in the care of the National Trust, are open from March 30th to October 31st, on Tuesdays, Wednesdays, Thursdays, Saturdays, Sundays and Bank Holiday Mondays, from 2–7 p.m. or dusk, if earlier. They lie on the B2114, a little way off the A23 (London-Brighton road), 1 mile south of the village of Handcross, 5 miles south of Crawley.

Penshurst, home of Elizabethan poet

Penshurst Place, the birthplace of Sir Philip Sidney in 1554, is a venerable building erected over a period of nearly 300 years starting in the early thirteenth century. In front and to one side of it the garden matches it admirably, and also has an air of antiquity, though it is mostly little more than 100 years old. It is an example of clever reconstruction of a sixteenth or seventeenth century garden, which gives the building a dignified setting.

In front of the house is a large, rectangular parterre with raised terraces on two sides. The parterre beds are large and of simple design, some outlined in Box and

Top The large rectangular parterre with raised terraces at each side, from which the design can be looked down upon. *Above right* The Lily pool has a figure and small fountain at its centre. *Right* An alley enclosed by Yew hedges and topiary.

filled with red Roses. Other beds are entirely planted with Box cut into low moulded slabs. A large circular basin for Water-lilies, with a central bronze statue of a youth, completes the design.

A Yew-enclosed alley cuts across the garden, and there are also orchards, a typical feature of the Kent countryside. At one point the Yew alley opens out into a large rectangle almost entirely filled by a pool enclosed by low, brick walls.

The entrance drive, at right

Top Looking towards the eastern wall of the garden at Penshurst Place, Kent. The garden walls date from the reign of Elizabeth I. *Above left* Prunus pissardii grown as standards in the cottage garden. *Above right* A glimpse through the Yew hedges.

---

angles to the Yew alley, passes between wide herbaceous borders which are backed by Apple trees, and between the drive and the great parterre are little orchard gardens each enclosed in Yew. It is the free use of fruit trees in a formal setting that makes the garden so unique and gives it a

Kentish flavour.

Penshurst Place is in Penshurst village on the B2176 road, 3 miles from the A26 road from Seven-oaks. Opening times (the dates vary slightly from year to year) are: Easter to the end of April, Saturdays and Sundays, 2 pm-6 pm; May adds Wednesdays and Thursdays, and June Tuesdays, too, 2 pm-6 pm; July to mid-September, Tuesdays, Wednesdays, Thursdays, Saturdays and Sundays, 1 pm-6 pm; Bank Holidays, 11.30 am-6 pm

The hand of time and man combine at Scotney

Nature and art combine in a scene of romantic beauty at Scotney Castle, Kent. The old castle dates from the fourteenth century, with later additions. Castle and moat, mellowed by time, are matched by the mature planted trees and carefully cultivated shrubs.

The medieval remains are concealed to the arriving visitor by the more modern front entrance to the house, which was built to the design of Anthony Salvin in 1837. From the terrace of the house you can see below the castle and gardens with fields and woodlands rising beyond. The approach is made all the more dramatic by a path leading down along the lip of a quarry.

The combined effect of the garden and ruins is the result of careful design and skilful planting over many years. A great deal of work was done by the aunt and uncle of the present owner,

Above The old boathouse at Scotney Castle, Kent. *Below left:* The combined effect of the garden and the ruins is the result of careful design and planting over many years, and the colour effect is very striking. Fine shrubs and Rhododendrons, in particular, are massed together in a woodland garden. Their profusion is offset by smooth undulating lawns. *Below right* The remains of the medieval castle and the moat mellowed by time are matched by some mature trees in the garden. *Over* The combined setting of the old castle and the more modern house reflected in the old moat.

Christopher Hussey, Esq, who has continued their efforts with great care and thought. There are masses of fine shrubs, such as the older hybrid Rhododendrons and Azaleas, now of great size. Other shrubs include Kalmias and Leucothoës, which were features of the typical 'American' gardens fashionable in the last century. The shrubs are offset by undulating lawns and mature specimens of such conifers as Lawson's Cypress, the Redwood and Incense Cedar, which rise majestically over the scene. A contrast is the remarkably large, spreading example of the so-called Dwarf Spruce, *Picea abies* 'Clanbrassiliana', owing its name to the first Lord Clanbrassil, who introduced it from Ireland about 1836. There are more recent plantings of Roses, perennial flowers and shrubs, and also an old ice-house, formerly used for storage.

Scotney Castle is 1 mile southeast of Lamberhurst on the A21 road. It is open Easter Saturday to the end of October on Wednesdays, Saturdays and Bank Holidays in the afternoons, and Sunday afternoons in October.

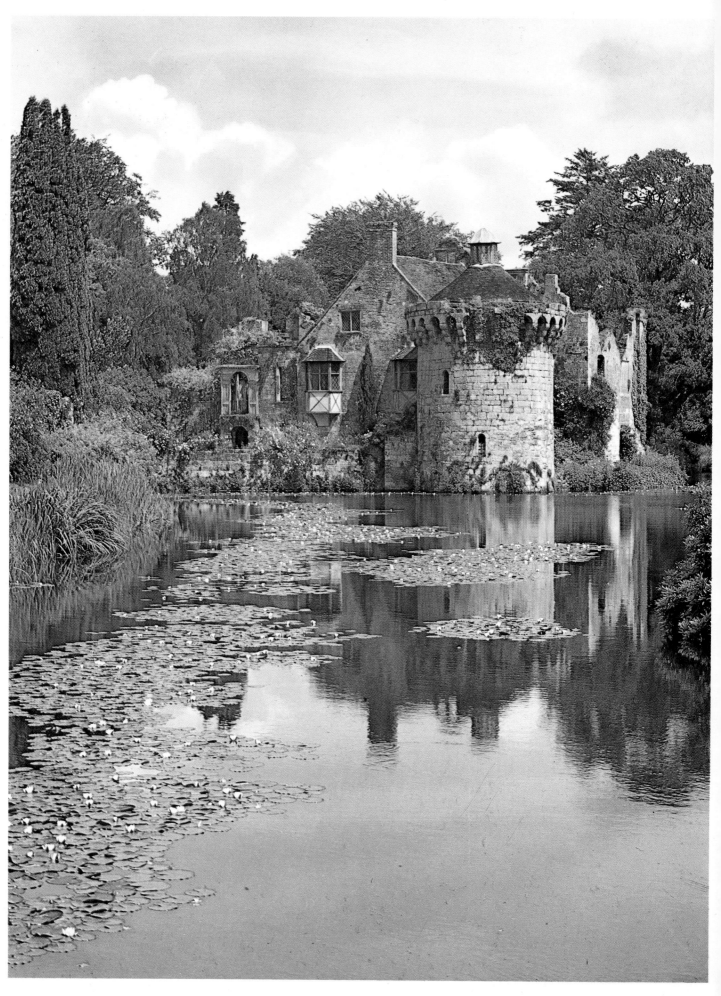

Chilham Castle, ancient trees in an historic setting

Chilham Castle, near Canterbury, Kent, is a Jacobean house built on the site of an ancient fort said to have been built by the Romans around 55 BC. The octagonal keep of a later castle still stands today in its own secluded garden.

The main gardens consist of a series of terraces connected by flights of brick stairs, with long, flower-filled borders. Each of these is backed by a wall supporting climbers of many kinds, some of which would be scarcely hardy in less sheltered places. Below the terraces is a large lawn along the edge of which are ten Yews, clipped to the shape of chessmen, and four Irish Yews. These stand beside a low stone wall overlooking the park, laid out by Lancelot 'Capability' Brown in the eighteenth century.

The grounds surrounding the castle are remarkable for their trees. There is an avenue of well-grown Limes, and another over a mile long consisting of Spanish Chestnuts *(Castanea sativa).* Here, too, can be found an Evergreen Oak *(Quercus ilex)* planted, according to legend, on the day in 1600 when building of the house was begun, fine specimens of the Blue Cedar *(Cedrus atlantica glauca),* Lawson's Cypress, an ancient Judas Tree *(Cercis siliquastrum)* its trunk now prostrate, and very large specimens of *Cotinus coggygria* the Wig Tree or Smoke Tree. Chilham also boasts one of the oldest Mulberries in England, the parent of many growing in Virginia, USA, grown from pieces taken there by one of the Digges family who became Governor of Virginia, and many other specimen trees. Against the south wall of the castle is a Wisteria, said to be the first to be planted in this country. This and a very large Banksian Rose, nearly 150 years old, completely cover the wall.

Chilham Castle, approached through Chilham village lies 5 miles south-west of Canterbury, just off the A252. The gardens are open on Thursdays, Sundays and Bank Holidays, from May to October and on Wednesdays also from June to October, from 2–6 pm.

Above right The Jacobean castle with neatly trimmed Yew hedges, through which scramble *Tropaeolum speciosum. Right* A massive Cedar, one of the many fine trees in the grounds. *Below left* Herbaceous borders, backed by brick walls, line the terraces. Climbing plants are grown against the walls and behind them can be seen some of the topiary specimens. *Below right* Looking from the terraces, over the topiary chessmen to the park beyond. *Over* Flights of brick steps of unusual design connect the various terraces.

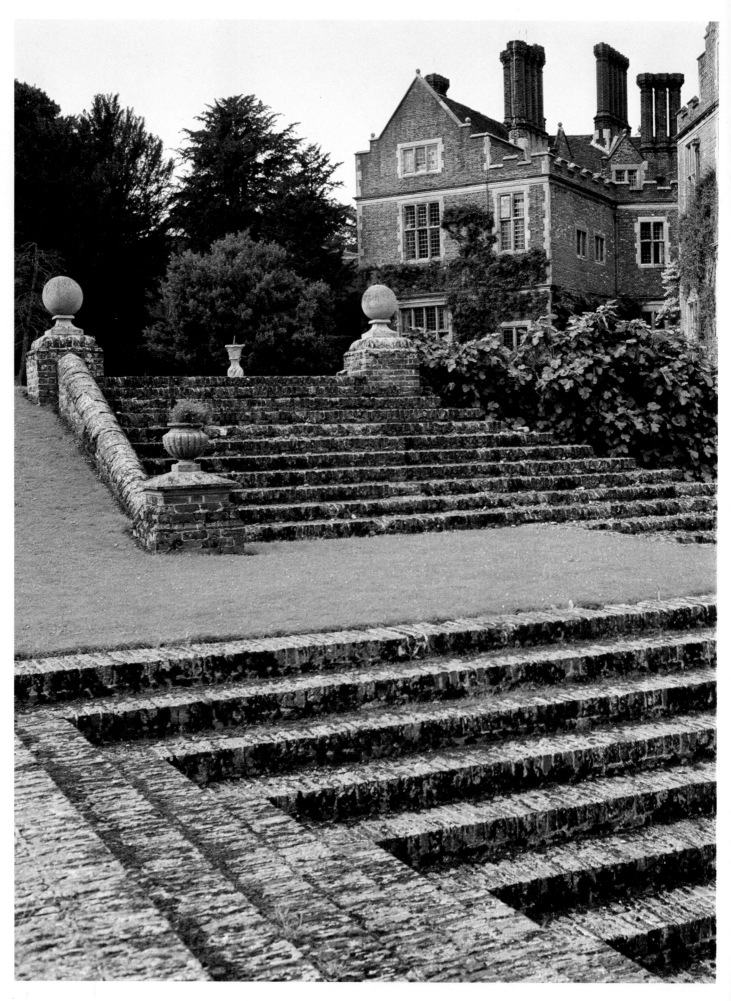

Chartwell, garden of the English countryside

It is interesting to compare the garden around Chartwell created by Sir Winston Churchill, with that of his great ancestor, Marlborough, at Blenheim Palace. The palace gardens at Blenheim are among the great and lavish spectacles of British gardens.

The magnificence of Chartwell is of another kind. It belongs to the wide and very English panorama of the countryside over which it looks.

The house is set towards the head of a steepish valley. It is unusually tall, looking back, in design, more to the English yeoman's home rather than the classical splendours of Blenheim. It stands on a platform which is irregularly terraced with some formality before merging into the landscape.

The entrance from the car park passes by some rock-work with a

Above: the rose garden in which the gold and yellow roses contrast with the blue of Nepeta mussinii planted round the edges.
Right: the walled rose garden in summer.
Below: an ornamental vine scrambles over a pergola to give a play of light and shade

small pool, shrubs and trees. Below the house there are pools in the valley supplied by a stream. They are the fish pond, whose golden orfe Sir Winston delighted to see, the swimming pool and the waters on which glide the famous black swans, originally a present from Australia. All these are carefully landscaped into the scene.

The garden proper lies around the house, whose height and walls are well used to shelter climbing and other plants. There are steps down to the grass below, but it is better to continue along the higher level through a series of interlinked gardens, moving on as

A view across the stream to the lawns and rose covered wall that surrounds the house just visible in amongst the trees

the view over the countryside, of orchards, fields and copses reaches out further and further. The most interesting part in high summer is undoubtedly what is now a large rose garden surrounded by the wall built by Sir Winston himself. Here is the walk of golden roses given to Sir Winston and Lady Churchill by their family as a golden wedding present.

It is pleasant to walk back on the grass immediately under the house. Good use has been made of the

lower terrace walls, while in the grass there are planted a number of interesting trees, such as a yellow-flowered horse-chestnut *(Aesculus octandra)* and silver maples *(Acer saccharinum)* natives of North America.

Chartwell is a National Trust property. It is two miles south of Westerham, in Kent, forking left off B 2026 after 1½ miles. The garden is open from April 1st to October 15th on Saturdays, Sundays and Bank Holiday Mondays, from 11 a.m. to 6 p.m. or dusk if earlier, and on Wednesdays and Thursdays from 2 p.m. to 6 p.m. or dusk if earlier.

Beauty Surrounds Sissinghurst Castle

In 1930 Sissinghurst Castle was derelict and was bought by the Hon. Sir Harold Nicolson and his wife, better known as Miss Victoria Sackville-West, the author. The rigid, formal garden plan was largely the work of Sir Harold; the planting, that of Miss Sackville-West. The partnership produced the subtle garden we now see, subtle in the grouping of plants, both for architectural form and colour. Particularly is this so in the white garden. Dominated by a silvery, weeping, willow-leaved pear, with the woolly leaves of lamb's ears, white-flowered irises, and an occasional gigantic Scots thistle, it is a highly original composition. But there are vigorous colour schemes too, particularly the plantings involving the old shrub roses. The walls shelter many climbers—a famous plant, the rose 'Mme Alfred Carriere', covers an enormous space. There is a herb garden, an old-fashioned cottage garden, and a large rose garden. And everywhere, at all seasons of the year, there are flowers. Sissinghurst Castle is half a mile off the A262, east of Sissinghurst village. The garden, which now belongs to the National Trust, is open daily, from April to October, from 10 a.m. to 7 p.m.

Left looking along the lime walk in April. *Below left* Yew hedges form the framework. *Below right* massed daffodils in spring, the Elizabethan castle in the background. *Over* the Herb Garden

Anglesey Abbey, a Fenland garden

The first Lord Fairhaven bought this old house in 1926 and made around it a garden on the grand scale, well suited to the flat Cambridgeshire landscape, with its wide horizons and spacious sky-scapes. Great use is made of sweeping vistas through trees, together with smaller, more intimate areas which are planted to give colour at varying seasons of the year. The garden is furnished with distinguished statuary, some of which comes from the original great garden at Stowe in Buckinghamshire.

On the sunny side of the house is a Rose Garden, the colours effective against its grey walls. A short walk around the east end of the building and northwards, is the Herbaceous Garden with its original semi-circular plan. From this, working across the end of the Arboretum with its rare trees, and passing the informal Quarry Pool, one reaches the quarter-mile long Emperors' Walk. Along it are set, against a background of dark and silver evergreens, twelve busts of Roman emperors. Half way down, a turn to the right takes one across the Arboretum to enter the South Glade, a sweep of grass with trees irregularly planted on either side. At its far end begins the Coronation Avenue, planted in 1937. Straight as a die, four rows of Planes and Horse Chestnuts on either side stretch for over half a mile. Intersecting this is a path which gives a surprise view of the Circular Temple, which is reached through a dark, bosky grove. It consists of a circle of large Corinthian columns guarded by two lions couchant. Turning right, down another wide, glade-like lawn, one again reaches the house.

Seasonal features are the Daffodil Walk, the Hyacinth Garden and the Dahlia Garden. There is also a Pinetum.

Anglesey Abbey, a National Trust property, is six miles north-east of Cambridge on B 1102. The gardens are open from 2 to 6 p.m. from Easter Saturday until the end of October, on Wednesdays, Thursdays, Saturdays and Bank Holiday Mondays.

Left The Circular Temple of Corinthian columns. *Above right* A well-placed statue with sundial. *Below* A stone temple with fountain. *Over above* A sweeping lawn looking toward the house. *Below* The Rose garden to the south west of the house.

Wrest Park— an Arcadian garden in Bedfordshire

The present house at Wrest Park, Bedfordshire, was built in an ornate French style early in the last century. The level garden viewed from the terrace was begun in 1706 and altered several times afterwards to fit in with changing fashions.

Immediately in front of the terrace are colourful parterre beds and an ornate marble fountain in the French style. In the distance across lawns, can be seen the Long Water, an original feature, which is a straight, formal canal

between high trees with a domed pavilion at one end. The best introduction to the garden is first to walk down to this attractive building. It was planned by William Archer, who also designed the monumental cascade pavilion at Chatsworth, Derbyshire. The pavilion at Wrest Park is decorated inside with trompe l'oeil work, consisting of figures and architectural decorations painted on the flat but made to appear quite solid-looking.

Entrances to a surrounding wood lead away from the canal. The wood contains a complex net-work of paths arranged for the most part geometrically, but including many that meander in an almost maze-like and apparently aimless way. By following them, all kinds of interesting discoveries

Left Part of the Rose garden at the side of the house. *Below, left* The bath house, recently restored, is in a secluded part of the garden. *Below, top right* A natural pergola of Lime. *Below, bottom right* The Chinese bridge.

are made. One terminates at a Roman altar, another with a vase. A third ends at a small summer-house, others lead to monuments. Emerging into the open stretches of water come into view—a narrow, irregular lake surrounds the whole woodland area. In one place it is crossed by a Chinese-style bridge built in 1874.

Nearer the house is a handsome Palladian bowling-green pavilion made in 1735, a fine orangery in the French manner built in 1836 and a rustic bath house and late eighteenth-century bridge.

Wrest Park, now the property of the National Institute of Agricultural Engineering, is at Silsoe, 10 miles north of Luton on the A6 Bedford Road, and the gardens are open Saturdays, Sundays and Bank Holidays from April to September, 2 pm–7 pm.

Right The formal canal with the pavilion beyond forms the access to the garden. *Below* The parterre with the orangery and bowling-green pavilion beyond stress formality.

Blenheim, a ducal landscape

The original garden at Blenheim was begun in 1705, designed by Henry Wise, gardener to Queen Anne, around the magnificent Palace designed by Sir John Vanbrugh, for John Churchill, 1st Duke of Marlborough. This garden consisted of a parterre near the house and a kitchen garden some way off. The parterre was in the baroque style, still to be seen in gardens in France, Germany and Austria, but nowhere else in the British Isles. It was laid out in swirling scroll-like patterns, studded with small bushes clipped into geometrical shapes.

Leading away from the house there are long, tree-lined vistas, crossed by Vanbrugh's triumphal arches.

Towards the end of the eighteenth century, fashion in garden design swung away from formality and 'Capability' Brown, in 1746 transformed the steep-sided valley by damming the little river Glyme to make the present great lake, one of the finest sheets of artificial water in Europe. The slopes of the valley were handsomely planted with trees in the style of the mid-eighteenth century.

Alas, at this time, the great parterre was destroyed, but to replace this the 9th Duke of Marlborough, in 1925, employed a French master of the old formal school, Achille Duchêne, to re-plan it and thus give us some idea of the original setting of the Palace.

Blenheim lies in the village of Woodstock, 8 miles north of Oxford, on A34. The garden is open from late March to October on Mondays, Tuesdays, Wednesdays and Thursdays but from mid-July to mid-October, daily, except Fridays; from 1–6 p.m.

Above: The Palace, with the modern parterre in the foreground. *Below:* The bridge designed by Sir John Vanbrugh and part of the artificial lake made by 'Capability' Brown. *Over:* One of the Bernini Fountains in the Water Garden.

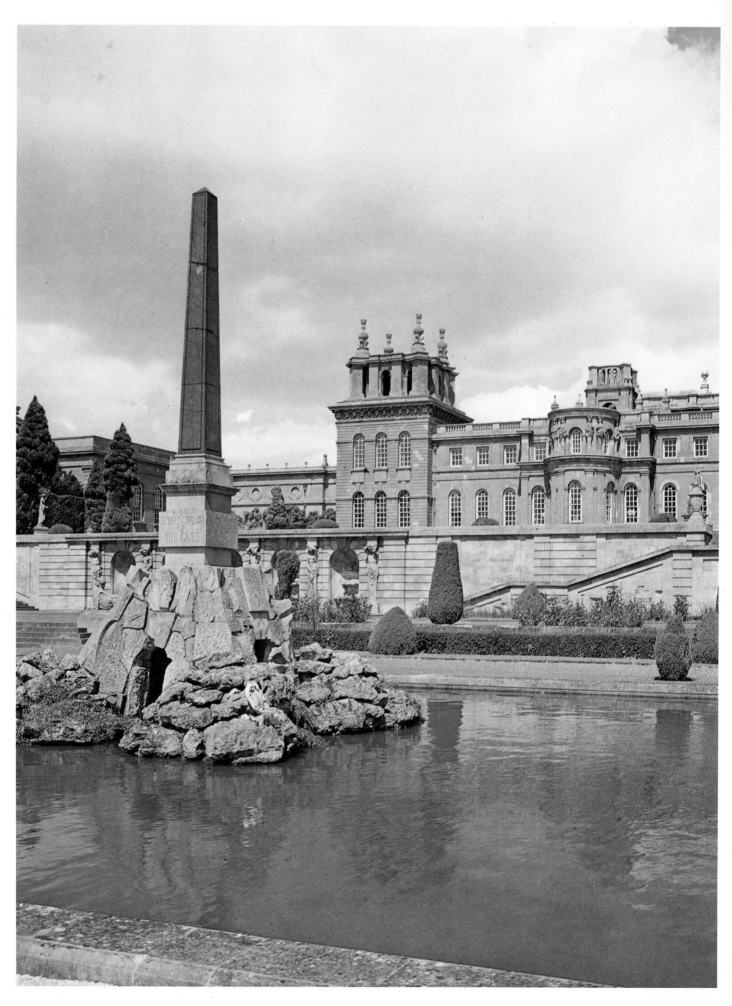

Charlecote, garden by the Avon

This estate belonged to the Lucy family from the twelfth century until it was acquired by the National Trust; the cleft oak palings which today surround it, and can be seen from the road, are of the type that has been used since medieval times.

The long, straight drive leading to the house is a magnificent Elm Avenue, some of the trees being of great age and girth, while others have been replaced over the centuries. Under the park trees on either side may be seen the herd of Spanish sheep and deer, which Shakespeare is supposed to have poached. At its end is the

pink brick gatehouse, which is much as Shakespeare knew it: at this point pause to look back at the majesty of the Avenue.

Within the courtyard is a pleasant modern garden, the gay statues, however, being a much earlier acquisition.

In the house, largely reconstructed in the nineteenth century, an item of interest to gardeners can be seen. It is a fine painting of the house and its elaborate seventeenth-century formal garden which was swept away by 'Capability' Brown when he landscaped the garden about 1760. One feature alone in it still exists—the Great Avenue. We can only assume that the Lucy of the day refused to have it felled to accord with the current fashion.

The long Grass Walks within a

Left The Tudor gatehouse at Charlecote Park, Warwickshire, built in pink brick, looks today much as Shakespeare knew it. *Below* Balustraded steps lead down to the River Avon, which meanders lazily through the park and its magnificent trees.

Above A shepherd and his dog and a shepherdess flank stone steps, the walls surmounted by flower-filled vases. *Below* The Tudor gatehouse.

Walled Garden, the elaborate Parterres and the curiously designed Double Canal from which arises a tall Summer House reached by a long narrow path with water on either side, have disappeared. The gardens by the house today, except for 'Capability's' Lebanon Cedars that sweep the grass, are of the nineteenth century, reaching down to the River Avon. All around are views of parkland which might well be the setting for a Shakespeare comedy.

Charlecote is four miles east of Stratford on Avon, on the north side of B4086. It is open from April to September daily, except Mondays (although open on Bank Holiday Monday) from 11.15 to 5.45. Bus 518 (Stratford, Warwick, Leamington, Coventry) passes the gate. The nearest railway station is Stratford.

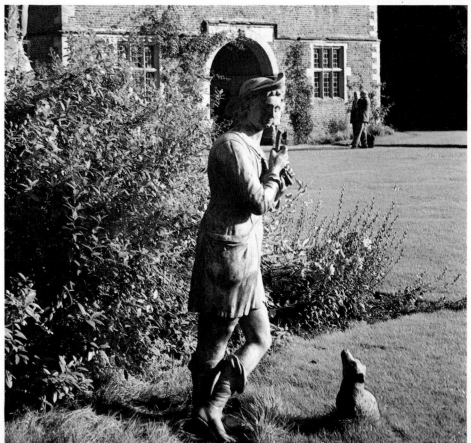

Compton Wynyates, a Tudor house in a modern garden

Lying hidden in a secluded Warwickshire valley, the house at Compton Wynyates is one of the most beautiful and picturesquely situated Tudor buildings in Britain. It has always belonged to the Compton family, and is the home of its present head, the 6th Marquess of Northampton. It was the birthplace in 1632 of Henry Compton, a most remarkable and forthright character who, when he became Bishop of London in 1675, made at Fulham Palace a most remarkable collection of trees and plants, many of them first introductions from eastern North America.

This glorious house has had a chequered career, having entertained royalty, been sacked by Cromwellians, been ordered to be pulled down by its owner to help pay his debts, but saved by a steward who ingored his instructions, and later rescued and restored.

Around it the ground is levelled below the now grassy remains of old terraces. The garden, of neither great size nor age, is rectangular. It is planted more or less regularly with evergreens clipped, however, most irregularly into a variety of shapes. Among them are grown herbaceous plants and roses, while a few standard trees give added variety. Thus a comparatively modern garden adds greatly to this historic house, and is seen to great effect when looked down upon from the grassy slopes that lead up to the surrounding woods.

Compton Wynyates is just north of B4035 Banbury—Shipston road, 10 miles west of Banbury. The house and garden are open from Good Friday to Easter Monday, then from April to September on Wednesdays and Saturdays and Bank Holidays from 2–6 p.m. on Sundays from June to August from 2–6 p.m.

The estate of Compton Wynyates lies in a valley on the Warwickshire border, and is seen at its best when looked down upon from the surrounding hills. *Over above* In summer herbaceous plants and roses add colour to the evergreens. *Below* The remarkable Tudor house stands amid clipped evergreens neatly shaped into an assortment of formal and unrelated designs.

Packwood House, a garden of contrasts

Packwood House is a timber Tudor building with later additions. It stands in typical Warwickshire countryside among fields, enclosed by hedges along which grow giant elms, interspersed with copses.

The garden is within a series of walled enclosures laid out in beds beautifully and gaily planted with modern plants. There is also a small, formal water garden made in the present century. These alone would make Packwood a delightful place to visit. But there is more to see of exceptional interest. There is, for instance, a long wall ending in what looks to be an unusual eighteenth-century gazebo. On examination, it proves to be nothing of the sort, but a small furnace house, whose purpose was to circulate hot fumes through flues within the wall, so warming it to prevent the frosting of fruit trees such as the peaches and nectarines that were once trained against it.

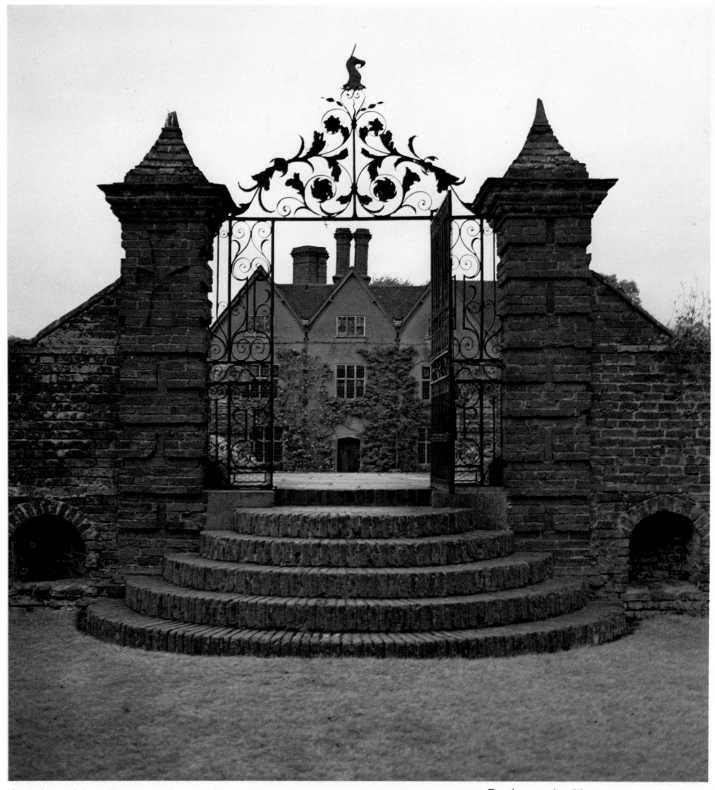

Another old wall across the garden has a fine gate. On passing through it and descending a semi-circular flight of steps, one sees a series of alcoves with arched tops on either side. These were made to shelter the old beehives, or skeps, when they were made of perishable straw.

Even more remarkable is the walk among large, neatly clipped yews leading to an old 'mound', a

Inside top: Spring bedding flanks the long path. *Centre:* The topiary garden, a group of clipped yews. *Below:* The furnace house that provided heat for the wall. *Above:* The gate with bee holes either side.

raised mound of earth whose yew-crowned top is reached by a narrow, spiralling path. There is a tradition—without, alas, much foundation—that this group of topiary represents the Sermon on the Mount.

Packwood House, a National Trust property, is open all year round on Wednesdays, Saturdays and Bank Holidays, and also on Tuesdays and Thursdays from April to September. It is reached by taking B4439 off A34 in the village of Hockley Heath, then after 1½ miles taking a minor road to the left; this passes between the buildings (identified by a sun-dial on one wall).

A thoughtful way with planning and planting

Burford House, on the boundary of Shropshire and Worcestershire, is in one of the most fertile parts of Britain, watered by the River Teme after it has left the border of Wales. The river flows past the garden. An early eighteenth-century red-brick building Burford House is the home of Mr John Treasure, who has made around it one of the most original and interesting of modern gardens.

It is essentially a plantsman's garden in which the contents must have great decorative value rather than botanical interest. Around the house there is a

Right Part of the stream garden at Burford House, Shropshire, a garden that makes full use of the water from the River Teme that runs through it. *Below, left* The paved garden and pool where the only splash of colour is from Petunias in the plant containers. *Below, right* The church tower beyond the shrub borders. There is a good collection of shrubs, tastefully planted in this garden now reaching its maturity.

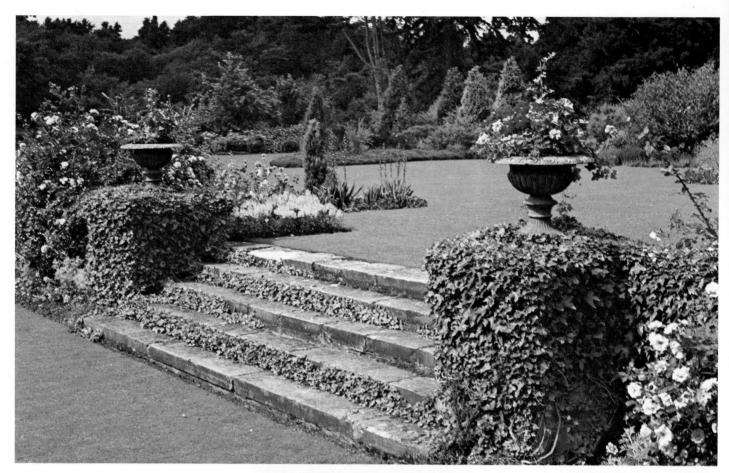

raised area treated formally. The planning of the garden itself consists of irregularly shaped beds set in wide areas of mown grass. These beds are planted, as is the whole garden, with most carefully selected shrubs and plants. Foliage and form are as important as flower, while labour-saving is very carefully considered. Many plants are grown in an unorthodox manner—for example, Clematis (of which there is a remarkable selection) are often found interweaving through other plants instead of being conventionally trained. The garden and its planting is of particular practical interest to those making small or moderate sized gardens.

Burford House lies off the Worcester—Ludlow A456 road, 1 mile west of Tenbury Wells and 9 miles east of Ludlow. The gardens are open daily from May to 12th October, 2 pm–5 pm.

Above The decorative use to which many plants have been put in this garden makes it one of the most interesting for plantsmen to visit. Ivy is used to cloth the steps that break up the levels of the garden. *Centre* The River Teme flows past the garden and provides a natural setting for the collection of plants assembled. *Below* Water from the river is taken to provide for the fountain.

The roar of traffic dies in the quiet groves of Weston Park

Turning off the roaring, crowded Watling Street, once a Roman road now a busy motor road, the visitor to Weston Park, Shropshire, soon finds himself winding through one of 'Capability' Brown's finest landscapes. The beautiful Restoration house, remarkable in that it was designed by its first owner, Lady Wilbraham, stands on a terraced garden. The broad, shallow terraces are decorated with topiary and ornamental vases. The final terrace takes the form of a balustraded arc, and on it grows an Oriental Plane, planted at least three centuries ago. Some 70 feet high, the branches spread over a circumference of 130 yards. From the terraces the view is over the park to a typical 'Capability' Brown lake disappearing among trees.

A fine walk can be had by sauntering through the long, narrow Temple Wood. Through it wind paths bordered by Rhododendrons, Azaleas and flowering shrubs above which rise magnificent Chestnuts, Oaks and Pines, terminating at one of the finest pieces of English garden architecture, James Gibbs's Temple of Diana. Within are an orangery, tea room and music room. Beyond this are the long, narrow Temple Pool and Gibbs's exquisite Roman bridge.

Nearer the house, the greenhouses and kitchen gardens will interest the practical gardener. The superb produce is grown by the organic method.

Weston Park is on the south of the A5 road at Weston-under-Lizard, 5 miles from Shifnal, 12 miles from Wolverhampton and 20 from Shrewsbury. The gardens and park are open at Easter, Sundays in April, spring and summer bank holidays and at midweek and week-ends from May to September at specified times.

Above The Temple of Diana designed by James Gibbs (1682–1754), the British architect. *Below* The fine Restoration house at Weston Park designed by Lady Wilbraham. *Over, above, left* A more formal part of the garden. *Above, right* Lawn and Rhododendron groves. *Below* The Oriental Plane with the house to the rear.

Fantastic Alton Towers

The remarkable garden Alton Towers, Staffordshire, hidden away in the picturesque valley of the little river Churnet was created by the immensely rich Earl of Shrewsbury in the opening years of the last century. He engaged celebrated architects, whose designs, however, he himself often modified. Begun in 1814 and added to by his successors, his fantastic garden remains almost unaltered today.

At the head of the valley below the lake is a statue of the earl within a small Grecian temple with the inscription: 'He made the desert smile'. Nearby stands a romantically conceived imitation of Stonehenge. In this part of the garden there is a series of ornate conservatories (within part of which is a stony grotto). On the right of the valley stands a red building originally intended to be a 'harper's cottage'.

An ornamental canal curves along the bottom of the steep valley. The sides of the valley are interlaced by a network of paths and steps moving from viewpoint to viewpoint and passing a rich variety of fantastic buildings,

Below, left The elegant pagoda fountain rising from a pool. *Below, right* Some of the wide variety of garden buildings and ornaments. *Over, above* Alton Towers seen across the lake, with some of the fine specimen trees. *Below* Part of the garden in summer; the conservatory is in the background.

fountains, colonnades, statuary and other garden ornaments. The trim lawns between are planted with flower beds, particularly of Roses, and there is a magnificent array of conifers and other ornamental trees.

In mid-June great masses of flowers of naturalised *Rhododendron ponticum* are in bloom.

However, an even more memorable sight is the exquisite Chinese pagoda rising out of a pond from the top of which a fountain plays, watering the surrounding trees. The garden is beautifully kept and secluded from the other popular features of the place. It can be viewed from an aerial railway.

Alton Towers, open daily, is reached through the well-signposted village of Alton, about a mile to the north of the village, off the B 5032 road, five miles east of Cheadle.

Chatsworth, a history of gardening

At Chatsworth, the ancient seat of the Dukes of Devonshire, is to be seen a history of gardening. The present house was begun in 1687. Around it, George London and Henry Wise, the most important garden designers of the day, laid out a vast and sumptuous garden in the style that Le Nôtre used for Versailles. Its elaborate design, lying among the sombre, remote hills amazed travellers. Traces of this garden and its fountains still exist, particularly the grand cascade (a slightly later

Above: The Great Cascade is a unique feature of the garden at Chatsworth. *Below:* The Cascade House from which the Great Cascade emanates through various sources.

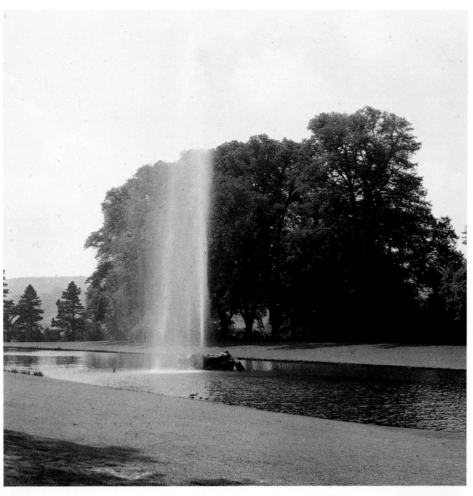

addition) that tumbles down the hillside. Next came 'Capability' Brown, who swept much of this away in the vogue for the natural landscape—and a lovely scene he devised in the park.

Chatsworth's great day was the arrival of an unknown young man on a spring day in 1826. The 'Bachelor Duke' had chosen him at a moment's notice to become head gardener. This was the first step to fame of Sir Joseph Paxton, later to design the Crystal Palace, based on the giant conservatory he built at Chatsworth for the Duke, which was demolished after the First World War. Much else of Paxton's work remains: there is his Emperor Fountain, throwing a jet 276 feet high; the camellia house—still looking 'modern' today and with some of the original camellias he planted growing within; there is his rock garden with its giant boulders and his arboretum with its many fine old trees surviving. Everything he did was on the most magnificent scale.

Today, we find also beds of roses, herbaceous plants and trees and shrubs of the latest kinds, all faultlessly cultivated, in addition to this historic gardening surviving from the past. A tour of the gardens, entailing a pleasant walk of something over a mile, takes one from the Orangery past colourful borders and the Sea Horse and Emperor Fountains, into the Azalea Dell, at its best in late spring, thence through the Ravine and into the Pinetum. The path continues past various ponds to the Aboretum and on to the Cascade House. From here it winds through the woods back to the house. At various points one can diverge to see the site of the Great Conservatory and other features of this historic garden.

Chatsworth lies a little way East of the village of Edensor, 6 miles North of Matlock, on A623. The gardens are open daily from early April to early October, on Mondays to Fridays from 11.30 a.m. to 4.30 p.m., on Saturdays and Sundays from 2 to 6 p.m., and on Bank Holidays from 11.30 a.m. to 6 p.m.

Above: The Emperor Fountain throws a single jet of water 276 feet into the air. *Below:* The narrow glass fruit cases designed by Joseph Paxton in the nineteenth century.

Haddon Hall, a terraced garden

The castle-like building of Haddon Hall sprawls over the end of a Derbyshire hillside with the River Wye curling below. A short flight of steps from the exquisite long gallery leads into a small, rectangular garden cut into geometrical beds.

This is the beginning of a very broad terrace with, on the right, a beautiful seventeenth century carved stone balustrade. To the left are hedges and minor terraces below the tree-clad rising slopes. To the right is a view down the

Above: The terraces are connected by this fine stone stairway. *Below left:* The broad lawn is surrounded by rose beds. *Below right:* A glimpse of the balustraded parapet to the top of the terrace long and beautiful south front of the house. The ground slopes steeply and interestingly in two directions, first along the side of the building and then, away from that, even more steeply to the river below. There is a wonderful view down on a series of small terrace-like gardens at different levels, linked by flights of steps and supported by walls.

The first flight is elegant and stylish, like the balustrade, and leads to a large rectangular lawn with a fountain at its centre. Great use of roses is made in this upper part of the garden. Below this the retaining walls are striking in their contrast. Upon them many plants are naturalised, others are trained against them, while interesting plants are grown in the beds at their base. Haddon Hall is 2 miles south-east of Bakewell and $6\frac{1}{2}$ miles north of Matlock on the A6 Buxton to Matlock road. It is open on weekdays (except Mondays) from April to September from 11 a.m. to 6 p.m. and on Easter Sunday and Monday, Whit Sunday and Monday and August Bank Holiday Sunday and Monday (Sunday openings from 2 to 6 p.m.)

Above: Full use is made of the walls. These shelter and support a wide variety of climbers and other shrubs which help to provide colour and interest against the grey stone

Below left: Many colourful plants grow in the cracks and crevices of the ancient retaining walls. *Below right:* A vigorous clematis grows over an old mullioned window

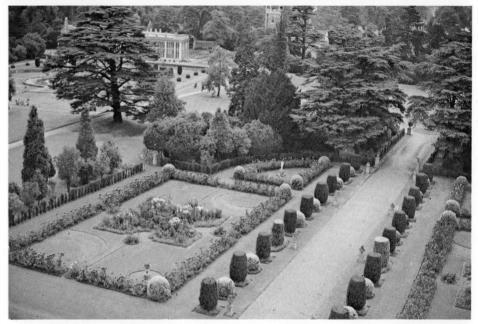

Rich, stylish and rare, Belton House

Belton House, Lincolnshire, home of the Brownlow family for 300 years, is one of the finest Wren-style houses built in Britain during the Restoration period in the seventeenth century. The garden has no affinity at all with the flat, bleak fenlands that form a large part of Lincolnshire. This is because the house stands on the slopes of a limestone escarpment.

The estate covers well over 600 acres. Massive and mature trees sweep in the form of a great avenue over the escarpment.

The gardens next to the house are formal. Northwards from the

Top, left A curved wall with a dripping fountain. Pelargoniums are grown in pots in the wall niches. *Top, right* Decorative wrought iron gates and screens lead to the stable block. *Centre and Right* Views of the formal Italianate garden with its carefully clipped trees.

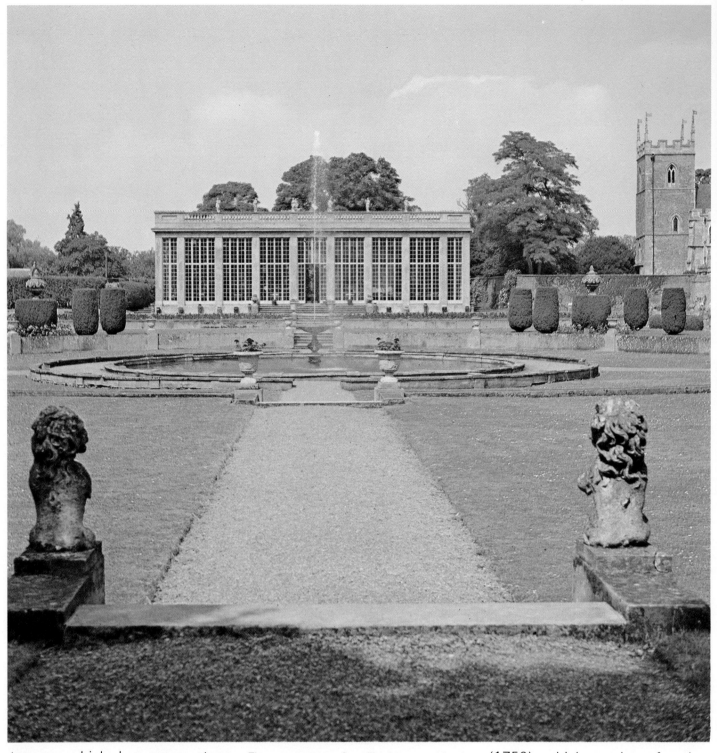

The orangery or Camellia house, with the ancient village church on the right.

terrace, which has many steps, there is a fine view down an avenue of Yews. The tall columnar Yews are flanked by lawns with Roses in Box-edged parterres terminated by two half-circular, Box-edged lawns.

A Cedar of Lebanon standing alone leads the eye gently to the great lawn and to a fountain and round pond setting off a classical-styled orangery, now a tea house decorated with growing Camellias.

At Belton the ancient village church forms a pleasing part of the landscape to the right of the orangery. In spite of changes many features at Belton recall the eighteenth-century landscape tradition, including the gothic ruin near the stables, a dried-up canal, a temple, a noble-looking sundial with figures of Father Time and Cupid and the magnificent avenue of trees leading from the east up the hillside to the Bellmount tower (1750), which consists of a giant arch capped by an upper storey.

To the south-east and east the park and woodlands in the distance are landscaped in the style of Lancelot ('Capability') Brown.

Belton is 2½ miles north-east of Grantham on the main Grantham–Lincoln A607 road, and is reached by a noble avenue of Elms which runs for a measured mile to the mansion itself. It is open between May and October every day except Friday, from 12 noon to 6 pm, and at Easter.

'Capability' Brown and Barry at their best

The magnificent estate of Harewood near Leeds, Yorkshire, provides outstanding examples of two entirely distinct types of garden, both typical of their period. One is a fine example of the English informal landscape of the late eighteenth century, the other is laid out on the lines of mid-victorian formality

In the 1840s, the then Countess of Harewood engaged Sir Charles Barry (who later laid out, in a similar style the gardens at Shrubland, Suffolk, and Trentham, Staffordshire) to design the formal garden. The present ornate garden front in an Italian manner is linked to the landscape by means of terraces in the same florid, yet undeniably grand manner. A large fountain plays on the main level, while statuary and the vases placed around it form decoratively formal beds, colourfully planted according to the season.

The lake designed by 'Capability' Brown, visible some way off over grass and backed by banks of trees (badly damaged some years ago by a gale, but now replanted) helps to make one of his best scenic effects. It is a delightful walk down to it, winding among old trees. Near one end of the lake a 'pleasure garden' contains a charming summer house 'guarded' by two stone owls.

Harewood lies on the A61 Leeds-Harrogate Road, 8 miles north of Leeds and 7 south of Harrogate. Opening times are every day from Easter Saturday to the end of September and Sundays in October, 11 am–6 pm.

Left, above A walk beside the lake, made by 'Capability' Brown, at Harewood House, Yorkshire. *Left, below* A cascade runs alongside the path planted with Azaleas, which leads to the lake. *Below* In front of the house is a colourful formal garden designed by Sir Charles Barry: The Victorian style contrasts with the surrounding informal garden. *Over, above* The formal design seen from the air. *Below* The Rose Garden provides colour at the edge of the lake.

Great formal vistas at Bramham

Why is it that Britain has no great formal gardens, architecturally designed, elaborated with terraces, canals, fountains, temples and long straight vistas on the same scale as those of Italy, France, Spain, Austria and elsewhere on the Continent? The answer is that in the early eighteenth century the English landscape garden was developed and fashion decreed that all the old gardens should be replaced by those in the new style of 'Capability' Brown. All went, except a very few that were somehow overlooked; one of these is the delightful Bramham Park, Yorkshire.

Robert Benson, later Lord Bingley, in about 1699 acquired the estate upon which Thomas Archer designed a house. Around this the garden was laid out. First came the long, straight woodland walks and the formal canals to which, up to about 1750, the buildings and ornaments were by degrees added.

The whole plan was devised in the form of simple geometry. At one point where rides intersect stands a magnificent vase, the 'Four Faces', from which there are views down a canal and up the long 'Cathedral Ride'. At one end of the broad walk in front of the houses is a temple in the Ionic manner from which there is a view in retrospect to the obelisk pond, from which water pours down an elaborate cascade. A delightful octagonal 'Gothic' temple provides a view which includes the pond seen from another aspect. There are, too, carefully designed vistas over the park.

The trees, mostly Beech, between which these walks passed, had become huge, their smooth grey trunks majestic. In February 1962 a devastating gale blew about 400 right over, their roots tearing up the ground. Many others were damaged. With great courage, the owners began clearing the wreckage, and then to replant. The young trees have grown well.

Bramham Park lies 6 miles south of Wetherby just off the A1 road. It is open between Easter and the end of September on Sundays and Bank Holiday Mondays and Tuesdays, 2 pm–6 pm.

Below One of the formal canals, dating from the early eighteenth century. *Over, above* The entrance gates, flanked by sphinxes and elaborate rusticated piers. *Below, left* The octagonal, 'Gothic' temple, one of a number of fine garden buildings at Bramham Park. *Below, right* One of the grotesque wall fountains through which water is fed into the canals.

Repton's landscape at Rudding Park

The Regency house at Rudding Park, Yorkshire, simple in design and beautifully proportioned, stands in a slightly elevated situation overlooking a calm and restrained landscape. In the foreground are aged trees in a park which has been skilfully placed against a woodland background, one of Humphry Repton's finest landscapes. The level and spacious view is an integral part of the design. The effect of flat trim lawns surrounding the house is relieved by fine old trees, some now of unusual form, and by charming vases and other garden ornaments.

As was usual at the time when such gardens were designed, the flower garden was concealed in a walled enclosure away from the views. Today, between it and the house, a transformation has been effected. Among the trees a woodland garden, with glades and grassy walks and ornaments has been created with great skill and

Right The Regency house looks out over wide lawns and well-grown specimen trees to a typical Reptonian landscape. *Below, left* An urn stands at a point where four grassy pathways meet. *Below, right* Double herbaceous borders, colourful for many weeks in summer, lead to the orangery.

taste. Masses of Primulas and intensely blue Poppies flower underneath the shrubs, which are a surprising selection—kinds one expects only in the moist, mild counties of the South West. The large-leaved Chinese species of Rhododendron and similar plants which grow so heartily, are also difficult to cultivate so far north.

Rudding Park is a short distance down a right turning off the A661 road three miles from Harrogate on the way to Wetherby. It is open daily, except Fridays, from Easter to October, 2 pm–6 pm; and Easter, Spring and late Summer Bank Holiday week-ends, and the Mondays and Tuesdays following them, 11 am–7 pm.

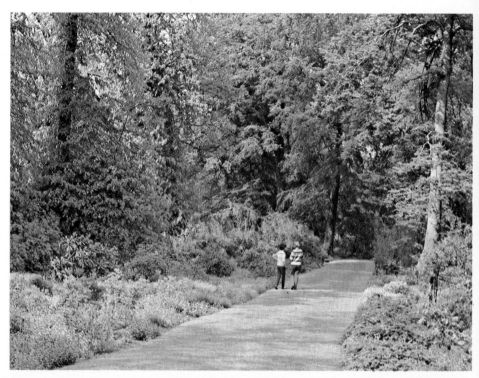

Right Blue-flowered plants add colour in this woodland glade after the Rhododendrons have finished flowering. *Below* A double border of Roses underplanted with *Alchemilla mollis* and other plants.

Harlow Car, Northern Horticultural Society's garden

Not far from the centre of Harrogate, on a site of 40 acres there has been formed, since 1948, a remarkable garden, finely landscaped and interestingly planted, the purpose of which is to demonstrate what plants and what types of gardening are possible in the bleak conditions of the north. Here, the Northern Horticultural Society is doing for its particular locality what the Royal Horticultural Society does at Wisley.

From the distinguished entrance gate, a long, wide grass 'broad walk' is bordered with shrubs and herbaceous plants. Behind those on the left are a very successful heath garden, well suited to the district, and a rock garden. Behind the beds on the right, at the top are the glasshouses, rose beds, and a trials area.

At the bottom of this walk is a stream, crossed at the point where there is a water garden. The opposite bank slopes up and is mostly wooded, with a glimpse of a portico of Doric columns (from the old facade of Harrogate's Spa Rooms). The woodland, extending a considerable distance on either side, is under-planted with many shrubs, and further away to the right there is a promising young arboretum.

These are but the principal features of a place of great practical interest to all northern gardeners and of delight to all throughout the year. The gardens are situated in Crag Lane, a turning off the B.6162, about a mile and a half from the centre of Harrogate, on the Otley Road. They are open daily, all the year, from 9 a.m. until sunset.

The Gardens of the Northern Horticultural Society at Harlow Car attract thousands of visitors each year. Highlights are 1 the Rose Garden, 2 the naturalised daffodils in light woodland and 3 the rhododendrons and azaleas. A collection of alpines is being established

The concept of the sublime— Castle Howard

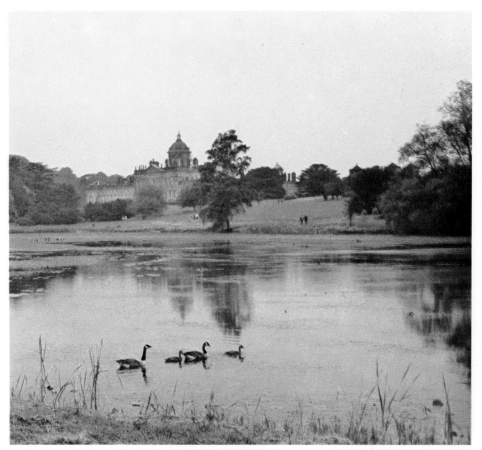

Horace Walpole, the eighteenth century connoisseur, described Castle Howard, Yorkshire, and its surroundings, as 'sublime'. The woods he said, were worthy of being each a metropolis of the Druids. The lawn, he called the 'noblest in the world'. Begun in 1699, for Charles, Third Earl of Carlisle, by Sir John Vanbrugh, the architect and dramatist, and Nicholas Hawksmoor, the architect, the building is surrounded by the first great landscape garden in the British Isles. It is quite distinct from the largest of the formal gardens of its day, but differs greatly from the typical 'Capability' Brown landscapes that followed.

The original long terrace extends from the east end of the house, with giant statues spaced out along its route. It terminates in Vanbrugh's 'Temple of the Four Winds'; beyond lies Hawksmoor's mausoleum—two landscape garden buildings probably, as beautiful as anything in Europe Walpole wrote of the mausoleum that it would 'tempt one to be buried alive'. Below, lies the lake, There are other objects of architectural interest, including a bridge, which lead the eye across the park.

Close against the house to the south is a simple formal garden with clipped hedges and statuary. In the centre is a large fountain with a Victorian style statue depicting Atlas supporting the globe. Other sculpture is well placed in the vicinity of the house,

Top Looking across the lake to the 'Mausoleum'. *Bottom* The great 'Atlas' fountain made about 1850. *Over, above, left* The 'Temple of the Four Winds', designed by Sir John Vanbrugh in 1724–26. *Above, right* One of the many pieces of statuary with a corner of the house beyond. *Below* The classical landscape as seen from near the 'Temple'; the bridge was designed by the architect D. Garrett in the 1740s, the 'Mausoleum' by Nicholas Hawksmoor in the 1730s.

including a boar in the garden against the west side. Some delightful flower borders have recently been added.

Castle Howard is reached by passing through magnificent avenues of trees lying just north of the A64 road, 6 miles west of Malton and 14 miles north-east of York. The grounds are open from Easter Sunday to October 5th on Tuesdays, Wednesdays, Thursdays, Saturdays and Sundays from 12.30 p.m.–6.30 p.m., and Easter, Spring and Summer Bank Holiday Mondays, 11.30 a.m.–5.30 p.m.

Studley Royal, a peaceful retreat

Studley Royal garden in Yorkshire is designed in the old formal architectural manner in a woodland setting of great picturesque beauty. Its origin is curious. John Aislabie, the owner of the estate, was Member of Parliament for nearby Ripon, becoming Chancellor of the Exchequer. He was involved in the 'South Sea Bubble' financial disaster, lost his office, narrowly escaped imprisonment, was fined £42,000, but remained well off, with his estates untouched. Presumably, as some consolation for his disgrace, in the valley of the little River Skell, he made this formal water garden, which has remained almost unchanged. It is approached from Ripon through a magnificent park. The design is entirely geometrical, the river itself is forced into a canal, and by its side are roughly circular-shaped pools overlooked by a Classically-styled temple. Standing by the temple, looking upstream, the valley seems blocked by trees. Following the path through their dense shade you come upon an unusual view. The river widens to form a small, half-moon-shaped lake. Beyond it, as a terminating focal point, is a spectacular tower dominating the ruins of Fountains Abbey. The whole aspect of the place has been changed from formal to romantic and picturesque. The reason is that though John Aislabie had always wished to acquire the upper part of the valley with its ruins, he was unable to do so. It was his son

Above Dominating the scene are the majestic ruins of the Cistercian monastery, founded in 1132 by 13 Benedictine monks from York, who joined the Cistercian Order. *Below* Two of the pools, with the Temple of Piety beyond, on a slight rise, tucked into the wooded hillside.

William, also an ardent garden designer, who obtained the property but in his time formality was out of fashion. There are several charming ornamental buildings, notably a banqueting house on the valley side.

The estate now belongs to the West Riding of York County Council, and is 4 miles south-west of Ripon and 9 miles north of Harrogate, west of the A61 road. The abbey and grounds are open all the year round at 9.30 am, except Christmas Day and Boxing Day and after 2 pm, on Sundays, from November to February.

Below, left In the foreground is the lead statuary piece known as The Wrestlers', beyond is a section of the long, straight canal, various other statues and in the distance the Temple of Piety. *Below, right* A part of the straight canal, running between smoothly shaven grassy banks. *Bottom* The canal finally runs over a weir and broadens out to become the River Skell again. The weir is flanked by rusticated piers and twin fishing lodges.

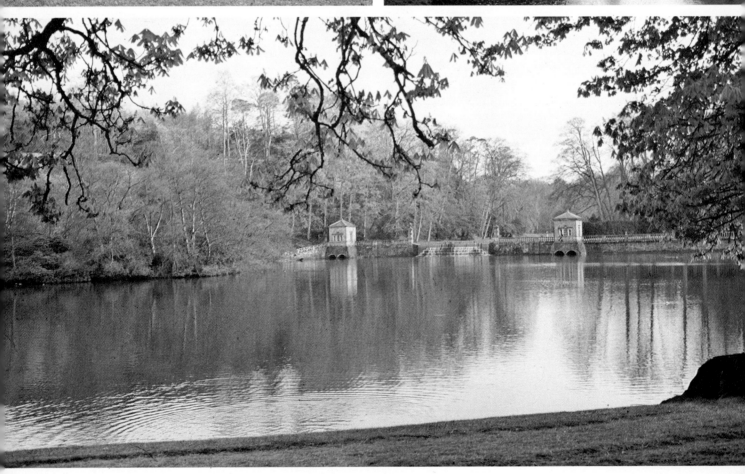

The terraced gardens of Powis Castle

Over, the view from the Castle to the Breidden Hills. *Below*, looking along the pathway which leads past the Orangery. *Bottom*, the Apple Slope, planted up with a wide variety of trees and shrubs, and the terraces above. *Bottom right*, looking across the terrace gardens.

Just outside Welshpool the red castle of Powis stands upon a crag, dominating the crossing of the River Severn and the old passage into Wales. In 1587 it was bought by Edward Herbert, a son of the Earl of Pembroke, whose son was created Lord Powis.

After the Restoration, the third Lord Powis repaired and added much to it, and it is believed that he was responsible for the garden's remarkable terraces, some 200 yards long, which drop down in four stages on to a lawn.

These terraces, which are among the very few remaining in a garden of that period, originally looked very different. Their huge yews were then small specimens, kept neatly clipped into cones and globes. Where we now look down on to a lawn, there was an elaborate garden of canals, fountains and statuary.

The sheltered terraces, facing south east, well above any frost pocket, are planted with a large, choice collection of shrubs, some on the borderline of hardiness. Opposite the terraces, there is the Wilderness, another collection of fascinating trees and shrubs. Beyond the garden to the south west, a Douglas fir rises above all its neighbours. More than 180 feet high, it is the tallest tree in the British Isles. Powis Castle may be approached on foot from High Street, Welshpool (A.490). Cars should turn up the road signposted to Waterloo (1 mile along the Welshpool-Newton road, A.483) and enter by the second drive gate on the right.

The gardens are open from May to the end of September, daily from 1-6 p.m. except Monday and Tuesday, but open on Spring and August Bank Holiday Mondays, from 10.30-5.30 p.m.

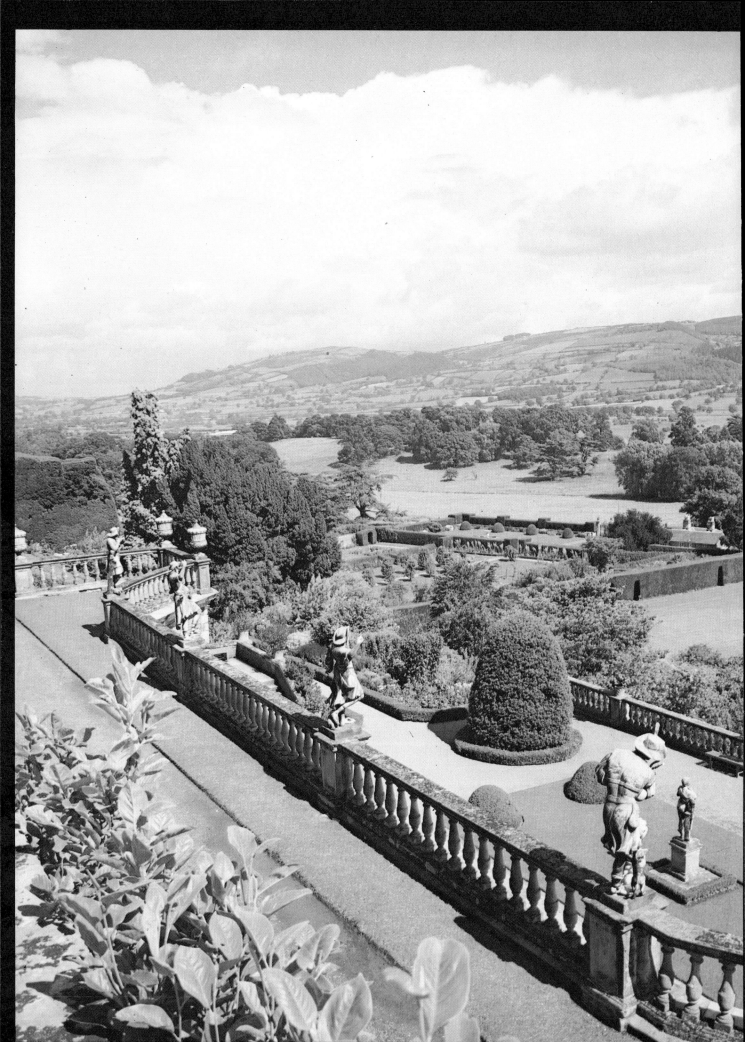

Bodnant the finest of British gardens

The garden at Bodnant, near Conway in North Wales, has been described as "the finest of contemporary British gardens". It is renowned all over the world and visited by tens of thousands of people each year. Its development was begun nearly a century ago by the first Lord Aberconway, and was continued by his daughter and later his grandson, the 2nd Lord Aberconway, who gave the garden to the National Trust in 1949.

Bodnant is now the home of the 3rd Lord Aberconway who is president of the Royal Horticultural Society. The whole garden covers nearly 90 acres and like many fine gardens is made up of a number of smaller ones. Around the house, and on the hillside immediately below, there are six great terraces, designed in the Italianate style, with lawns, pools, rose gardens, great trees and other features such as garden statuary and urns.

The terrace walls and the pergolas are clothed with plants, many of them rare, others tender but flourishing in this mild, moist climate.

On the canal terrace at one end of a long, narrow, formal pool stands the Pin Mill, originally built about 1730 at Woodchester in Gloucestershire. It was once used for pin manufacture, hence its name, but was moved to its present site just before the last war and is now used as a garden house. At the other end of the canal is an open-air theatre built in the Italianate style.

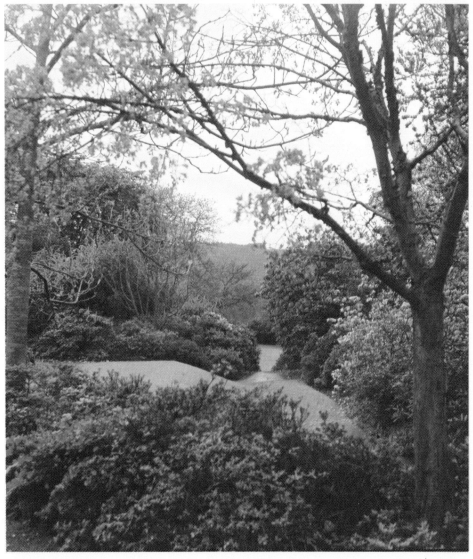

Top, looking over the Italianate terraces to the Snowdon range. Right, a glimpse of the woodland garden in May. Over, the Pin Mill at the end of the Canal, seen from the open-air theatre.

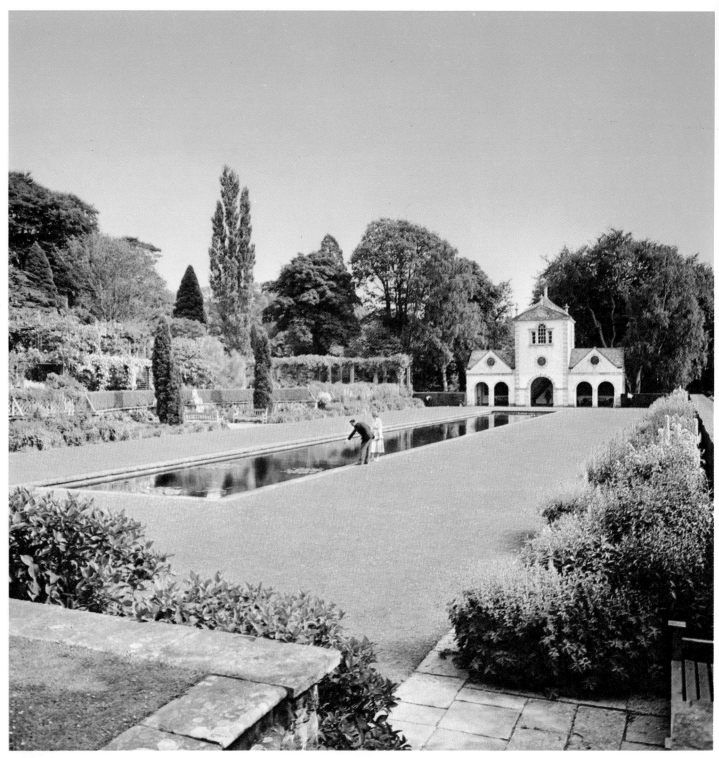

Leading from the terraces, there are walks lined with rhododendrons for which Bodnant is famous, with camellias and with flowering trees. They take you to shrub gardens and down to the glory of this garden, the Dell. This is a glen in which tower many fine specimen trees, especially conifers, many of them planted nearly a century ago and through which runs the little river Hiraethlyn, its power once used to turn a flour mill. From a bridge which spans the river there are fine views along the Dell.

The banks are planted with masses of rhododendrons, particularly of the azalea section, camellias, enkianthus and other shrubs. Round the rocky pools, there are primulas and other moisture-loving plants.

This National Trust garden is open from April 1st (or from Easter Saturday if Easter falls in March) until October 31st, on Tuesdays, Wednesdays, Thursdays, Saturdays and Bank Holidays, from 1.30 to 4.45 p.m.

Members of the National Trust and Fellows of the Royal Horticultural Society are admitted free on presentation of their membership cards. Bodnant is on the east side of the Conway Valley some four miles south of Conway and seven miles from Llandudno and Colwyn Bay. It is seven miles north of Llanrwst, on the A496 road.

Visitors are admitted only at the main entrance on the Eglwysbach road, where there is a car park.

The garden is supervised by Lord Aberconway, V.M.H. for the joint committee of the National Trust and the Royal Horticultural Society.

Branklyn, a plantsman's garden

Branklyn, is a remarkable garden, as exciting for the plantsman as it is for the amateur. The size of the garden is now two acres. In 1926 when the late John and Dorothy Renton built the house it was about a third of the size and contained but few plants and those of no great outstanding interest. It was some years before they became keenly interested, but their subsequent enthusiasm led to the gradual acquisition of an adjoining orchard until necessity or discretion called a halt when the garden had reached its present size. The

Above A number of old trees have been enveloped in Roses and Clematis, and add to the background colour effect of the garden at Branklyn. *Below* A path runs between borders richly planted with shrubs and perennials.

things which interested them most were alpines and ericaceous plants. To accommodate these two large scree beds were made and in due course peat walls in the shadier parts of the garden for the many gaultherias, cassiopes, vacciniums, dwarf rhododendrons and a multitude of other plants which prefer these conditions. In dealing with a small area the selection of plants is particularly important. At Branklyn each plant had to earn itself a place; rarity or cultural difficulty alone did not qualify. The same care in selection was applied to the trees and shrubs which now provide background and screening for the garden. They also contri-

The collection of plants amassed at Branklyn is remarkably wide, and all are peat loving. The garden was built up during the life-time of Mr and Mrs Renton, and on their death given to the National Trust for Scotland.

bute much to the atmosphere, which is further enhanced by a number of old apple and pear trees through which scramble Roses and Clematis and a notable plant of *Hydrangea petiolaris*. Where you have a choice visit the garden in late May, June or July when the majority of alpines are in flower and when Meconopsis, Iris, Rhododendrons and Lilies are at their best. The majority of shrubs and trees flower well during these

months, although Hoherias, Hydrangeas, Shrub Roses and of course herbaceous plants continue well into August.

When Mr and Mrs Renton died, the property was offered in the will of John Renton to The National Trust for Scotland, in whose care it now rests.

Branklyn is within the City of Perth. It lies on the east side of the River Tay a quarter of a mile south of Queen's Bridge on the Dundee road — one of the many gardens that flourish on the 'cold' east side of Scotland. Opening times are: May to September, Mondays to Saturdays, 2 pm-5 pm; Sundays 2 pm-6 pm.

Brodick, garden on an island

The Isle of Arran lies in the Firth of Clyde. It is mountainous — Goat Fell rises to over 2,800 feet — though the low ground by the sea is very fertile: the Gulf Stream gives mild conditions counterbalanced by destructive winds.

By the sea on the eastern side stands Brodick Castle, a typical Scottish baronial building with mountains as a back-drop. Immediately in front of the building there is a long grass terrace with magnificent views. This leads to an old walled garden containing six rectangular lawns between which are pergolas covered with wisteria and a good selection of

Right Brodick Castle is a typical Scottish baronial building standing high on the Isle of Arran. *Below* In spring the Primulas make a wonderful display of colour. *Below right* The effect of the warm Gulf Stream allows many tender plants to flourish here.

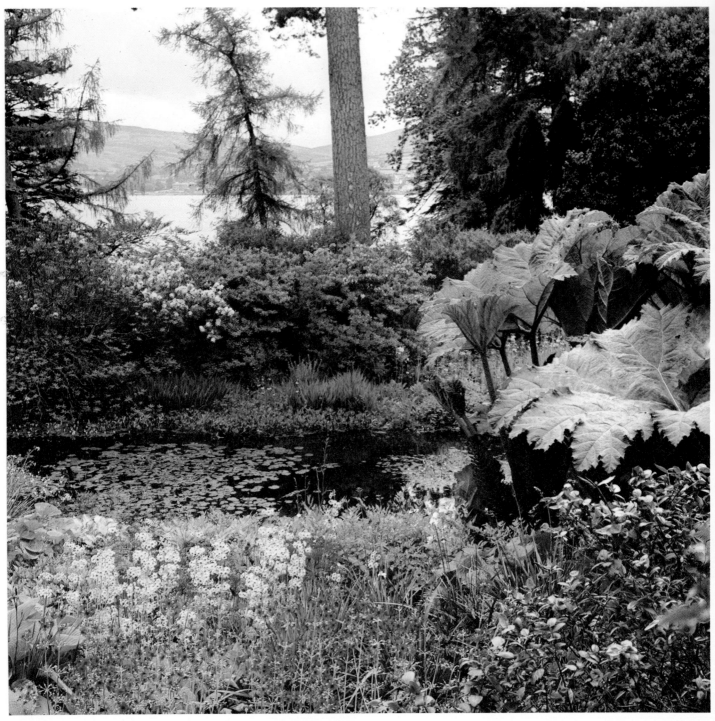

Climbing Roses. Against three of its sides are borders of herbaceous plants as well as, for example, tender Fuchsia hybrids.

Below that, separated from the sea by giant bushes of *Rhododendron ponticum* which give protection against storms, is a woodland walk.

In the thirty years before her death in 1957, the Duchess of Montrose cleared and converted ancient scrub to create the famous garden we now see. Bays were cleared to shelter the sensationally large-leaved and tree-like Rhododendrons, many of which were

The present garden was created by the Duchess of Montrose, and upon her death in 1957 the estate was given to the National Trust for Scotland. The rock and water garden have been made since that time and many more varieties of Rhododendrons introduced.

introduced from western China and Tibet by collectors such as Forrest and Kingdon-Ward. With an annual rainfall of some 70 inches a year, these giants are so at home that they seed themselves.

More recently a rock and water garden have been added and even more Rhododendrons introduced from the collection of Sir James Horlick on the island of Gigha.

Brodick also boasts flowering trees and shrubs of all kinds, a 30-foot hedge of Crinodendron, drifts of Primulas of many kinds and Meconopsis in blue, yellow and pink, and water-loving Irises.

Now in the care of the National Trust for Scotland, Brodick Castle and its 60 acres of garden are open to the public at Easter weekend, then daily, except Sundays, from May to September. The gardens are open from 10 am–5 pm and the castle from 1–5 pm. Ferry services run from Ardrossan and Fairlie to Arran and there is a bus service to the castle gates.

Crathes, a garden in a romantic setting

The tall grey building with its fanciful tower, so typical of Scotland, rises among the wooded coppices above the River Dee. It has a venerable history of gardening, with lime tree walks and yew hedges dating back to the eighteenth century. The remarkable garden we now see,

Top   A view of Crathes Castle tower from the garden with its lime tree walks and yew hedges dating back to the eighteenth century

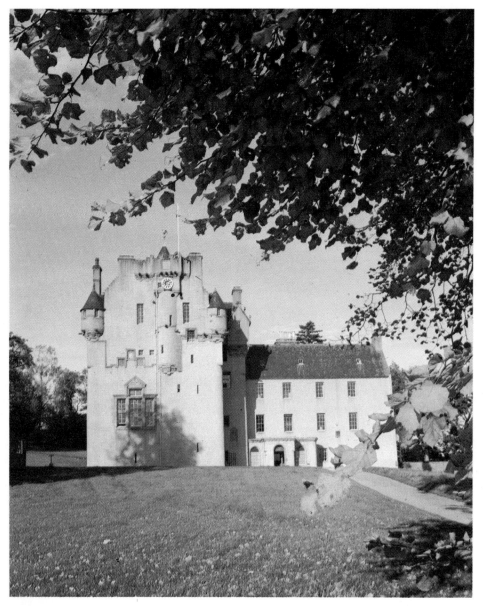

making splendid use of a romantic setting, is largely the work of Sir James Burnett of Leys.

The grounds are divided into a series of rectangles, some of which are framed with old yew hedges, where choice and unusual, and sometimes difficult, plants will thrive.

From the range of greenhouses runs the long path to the doocot, or dovecot. The border beside it includes the California Laurel, *Umbellularia californica*, the Tibetan Cherry with bark like highly polished mahogany, and the large Tree Peony, *Paeonia delavayi*, with dark blood-red flowers.

The approaches to the castle and the avenues are of particular interest, planted as they are with magnificent old Scots Pine, Douglas firs, the rare Japanese Lacquer Trees, Antarctic Beeches from South America and New Zealand, the true Chinese Cotton Tree, the weeping Brewer's Spruce, and a survivor from prehistoric time, the Dawn Redwood. Crathes Castle, a property of the National Trust of Scotland, lies in Kincardineshire, a little north of the A93, about fourteen miles west of Aberdeen. The garden is open daily throughout the year from 9.30 a.m. to dusk.

The grounds of Crathes Castle are divided into a series of rectangles that are more or less regular. Though planted with irregularity to provide an effective arrangement of colour, interest is maintained throughout the year

The garden pride of the County Down

The house and garden at Rowallane, Northern Ireland, lie not far from the sea in gently undulating country with Beech and Pine woods. The rainfall is typical of County Down, where they assure you it rains most days but seldom for long. Plants that like high humidity and dislike summer droughts thrive. Surrounding trees give good protection from gales and the soil is acid.

Driving up the long entrance drive shows that here is a garden full of good trees and shrubs. The late Hugh Armytage-Moore, who had a flair for design and the effective placing of his plants, began making the garden in 1903. He was a clever propagator and seed raiser just when there was a flood of new arrivals from western China, sent by E. H. Wilson, George Forrest and other successful collectors. The visitor can enjoy many mature specimens of these new introductions. Near the house are two gardens enclosed by high walls, against which are trained some rather tender shrubs, such as Azara and Tricuspidaria.

Leaving the formal gardens, you follow wandering paths in a series of distinctive areas each enclosed by low stone walls. The Spring Garden is full of Azaleas and Rhododendrons—both old and new kinds—making a brilliant display, with other trees and shrubs giving an equally rich autumn colour. The Old Wood is interspersed by great outcropping slabs of rock and Scots Pines, and a small stream provides moisture for

Above: The name Rowallane is derived from a Celtic word meaning outcrop of rock, and this garden near Belfast has been made in such a location. The careful planting assures colour interest throughout the season. *Below:* One of the wall gardens, where many tender and interesting plants thrive.

Above left: The natural outcrop of rock provides a setting for a rock garden in which many unusual plants are to be found. In spring this garden is at its height of attractiveness. *Above right:* Rowallane has a remarkable collection of Rhododendrons and Azaleas and spring-flowering shrubs. *Below:* The artistry in the planting and the selection of plants was the hand of the late Hugh Armytage-Moore, a successful raiser of plants.

many of the smaller Rhododendrons, Rodgersias and Lysichitums. Everywhere there is a feeling of space, and a sense of surprise on seeing little-known plants—always of great garden merit and placed with great skill. There are also many fine specimens of uncommon trees, including Nothofagus, species of Prunus and Malus, Abies and Picea.

Rowallane is a National Trust property, 11 miles south-east of Belfast and 1 mile south of Saintfield village west of the A7 road to Downpatrick, opening daily April–June, 10 am–6pm, evenings (fine) 7–9 pm; July–October, Wednesdays, Saturdays, Sundays and Bank Holiday Mondays, 10 am–6 pm.

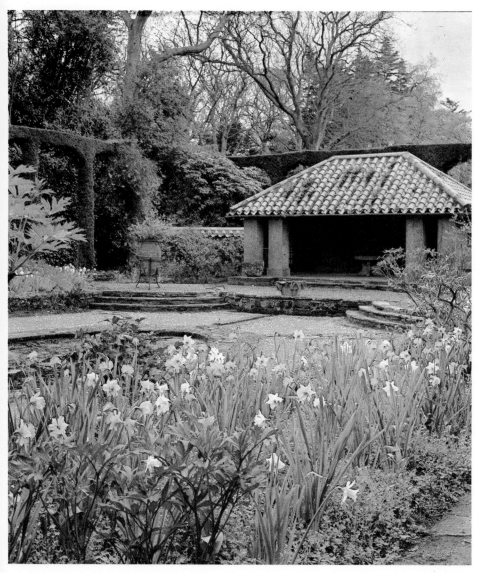

Mount Stewart, a fine Ulster garden

Mount Stewart is one of the last British gardens to be laid out in the grand manner. Although it already looks mature, the planning and planting of its 78 acres were not begun by its creator, the 7th Marchioness of Londonderry, until 1921.

Almost an island, lying between two loughs and subject to the mild airs of the Gulf Stream, this garden boasts a wide range of plants that would elsewhere be tender. Making use of the visual beauties of the scenery, formality and informality are combined in a series of gardens surrounded by woodland and inter-woven with paths, lavishly planted with Rhododendrons, Camellias, Eucalyptuses, Magnolias and a selection of other rarities.

Only some of the gardens can be described here. That on the south side of the house, and running its length, is formal and in the Italian manner, having as its main inspiration the villas Gamberaia and Caprarola, but employing planting material that was unknown in the days when these famous Italian gardens were made, the parterres containing both rare shrubs and herbaceous plants. The garden along the west side of the house, with a pergola, is otherwise sunk and enclosed by Macrocarpa hedges.

To the north lie the woodland and waterside walks, with at one point an outcrop of rock around which was made a natural rock garden.

Another interesting feature, of particularly national interest, is the

Above The gardens at Mount Stewart consist of a series of gardens, some formal and others informal, skillfully created by Lady Londonderry, 7th Marchioness of Londonderry, after the first World War. The Spanish Garden in spring marries formality with naturalised planting. *Below* The Tin-N'An Oge or Burial Ground set out in a formal manner with paved paths and a small formal water garden at the centre.

Shamrock Garden. It is paved, and the plan is that of a Shamrock. At its centre is a bed, the shape of the Red Hand of Ulster planted with the red-foliaged *Iresine herbstii*. The surrounding hedge carries a hunting scene in topiary work.

Mount Stewart is a National Trust property. It lies on the eastern shore of Strangford Lough, 5 miles south-east of Newtownards, 15 miles east of Belfast on the north side of the Belfast-Portaferry road (A20). It is open from April to September on Wednesday, Saturday, Sunday and Bank Holiday Monday from 2—6 pm.

Above The Spanish Garden set out in formal manner is a sunken garden. Here the formal pool lies below an impressive flight of steps which leads down from the southern facade of the house, bordered by a massive hedge. *Below* The Shamrock Garden is unique in that it is laid out in the form of a Shamrock. It is paved and at the centre is a bed the shape of the Red Hand of Ulster, planted with Iresine herbstii.